PORSCHE
356 AND RS SPYDERS

Gordon Maltby

Photography by Dave Friedman
& Gordon Maltby

Motorbooks International
Publishers & Wholesalers ®

To my father and his car stories—another car story

First published in 1991 by Motorbooks International Publishers & Wholesalers, PO Box 2, 729 Prospect Avenue, Osceola, WI 54020 USA

Motorbooks International books are also available at discounts in bulk quantity for industrial or sales-promotional use. For details write to Special Sales Manager at the Publisher's address

Library of Congress Cataloging-in-Publication Data
Maltby, Gordon.
    Porsche 356 & RS Spyders / Gordon Maltby.
      p.   cm.
    Includes index.
    ISBN 0-87938-551-0
    1. Porsche automobile—History. I. Title. II. Title: Porsche 356 and RS Spyders.
TL215.P75M35 1991
629.222'2—dc20   91-31168

Printed and bound in Hong Kong

On the front cover: *A 1957 Carrera 1500GS sunroof owned by Hank and Phyllis Godfredson of Bloomington, Minnesota. This car, originally delivered to Swiss Trading, Bangkok, Thailand, soon made its way to Minnesota where it was used in rallys by Lloyde Woolery and went through a number of owners before entering into a racing career late in life. Along with the original silver, the red stripe scheme often seen on early Carreras was chosen by the Godfredsons when they restored the car in 1986. It is now used for vintage racing and has appeared in Porsche events around the country.*

On the back cover: *Top, a freshly-restored 1956 Speedster photographed near the Blue Ridge Parkway in North Carolina in September 1990. Center, an RS60 Spyder approaching a turn at the Chicago Historic Races at Road America, Elkhart Lake, Wisconsin, in July 1991. Bottom, a 1957 A coupe in Aquamarine blue with a red interior. The car was restored by Californian Gary Emory in the style of a lightweight GT with Speedster seats, plexi windows, roll bar, polished hubs and wide rims. Photographed by Hal Thoms at Casablanca Estate, California in May 1989.*

On the frontispiece: *A line of Porsches leads the way through a downhill corner in a March 1963 race at the Los Angeles Dodger Stadium, with Dave Jordan's Speedster in the lead. Dave Friedman*

On the title page: *Ken Miles' RSK leads the field at the Kiwanis Grand Prix at Riverside in July 1959. Dave Friedman*

Contents

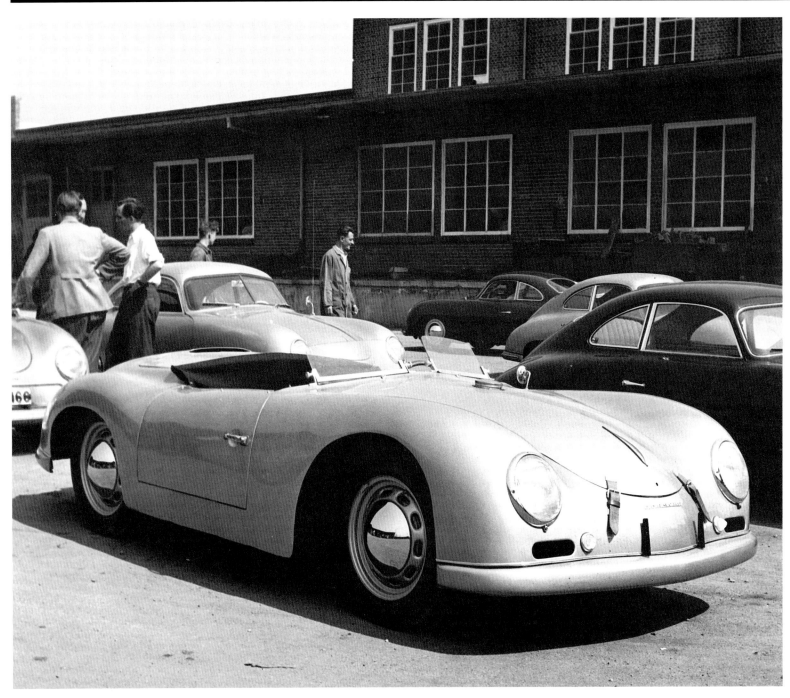

Zuffenhausen, 1952
Heinrich Sauter's lean and clean roadster is seen in the courtyard of Reutter's Zuffenhausen works in 1952. External gas filler, hood straps and racing windshield proclaim its competition intentions. Tom Countryman

Acknowledgments

To the many people who have given their time and energy in contributing to this book, my sincere thanks. Special thanks to Klaus Parr and Olaf Lang of Porsche AG, Dennis and Dave Aase, Jim Barrington, Dave Friedman, Hank Godfredson, Brett Johnson, Otis Meyer of *Road & Track*, William Miller, Bo Olson, Harry Pellow, Fred Senn, Rob Stuart and Stoddard Imported Cars, Hal Thoms, Betty Jo Turner, Jim and Steve Wellington, Tom Warth, George Wilke, Tom Countryman and the many 356 owners whose cars appear on these pages.

Del Mar, California, April 1963
*Two Speedsters sandwich a Sunbeam through the corners at Del
Mar.* Dave Friedman

Introduction

The story of the Porsche automobile does not begin with the first vehicle that carried the name. When the initial Type 356 sports car appeared for testing on the mountain roads outside of Gmünd, Austria, in 1948, it was only the latest in a series of Porsche mechanical creations that had already spanned nearly half a century, and to take up the tale at that point would be to start in the middle. The Porsche name had been well known in automotive circles for as long before the car appeared as it has since, and it can be argued that the same vehicle *without* those seven letters on its nose would never have engendered a sixteen-year production run of 76,000 cars. Indeed, without either the reputation of Ferdinand Porsche or the determination of his son Ferry and daughter Louise, their postwar car-building venture might have quietly died.

Beginning at the turn of the century, Ferdinand Porsche had become known as a premier automotive designer. From the pinnacle of success in 1930s Grand Prix racing to the ruin of postwar Germany, the fortunes of the family and the company had ridden the fast-moving currents of politics and war, which by 1948 had left them in an Austrian backwater. Equipped with little more than a few machine tools, the men working in Gmünd were able to begin building a new type of car, and to begin rebuilding the company.

The basic design of what would become the Porsche was laid down by Ferdinand Porsche and his staff during the mid 1930s in the form of a simple and economical conveyance—a "people's car." That the same layout would continue in production for decades and be successfully adapted to a high-performance sports machine is a tribute to the professor's conviction that with superior design, "inexpensive" does not have to equal "cheap." He initiated and pursued the Volkswagen project as a personal crusade while other German car manufacturers looked on in amusement and amazement. It is ironic that he never lived to see the overwhelming success of that car and another bearing his own name. Carrying on his dedication to excellence was his son Ferry.

Having worked at his father's side for many years with a wide variety of responsibilities, Ferry Porsche was talented and well trained for the work of designing automobiles, but to overcome the daunting obstacles he faced in postwar Austria required much more. The first Porsche sports car and the fifty more that emerged from the old mountain sawmill in Gmünd were a testament not only to the skill of his staff, but to his persistence in pursuing the dream he shared with his father.

Only a few short years after the first Volkswagen-based Porsches entered the marketplace, the company produced an elegant and sophisticated powerplant based on the fifteen-year-old VW engine. With four shaft-driven overhead camshafts, roller-bearing crankshaft and a displacement of just 1.5 liters, the new motor was a technical achievement that reflected the glory days of the Porsche Design Bureau. The era of this Type 547 engine and the racing Spyders it powered would parallel the development of the first series of Porsche road cars, and for a decade, the combination of the four-cam in a 356 body would become the ultimate street Porsche, the Carrera.

From turn-of-the-century electric carriages to the last of the Spyders, these machines and the men who designed, built and raced them are part of a fascinating story that spans over half a century across many continents. And if the story of the 356 does not begin in 1948, it also does not end in 1965, when the last of the line left the factory. Enthusiasm for the cars has grown tremendously in the twenty-five years since they were current models, and today the first series of Porsche sports cars are well established as milestones in the annals of automotive history.

Exelberg, Austria, 1902
Ferdinand Porsche demonstrated the Mischwagen, which featured a gas engine powering DC generators in the hubs. Porsche won his hillclimb class in the process. Larger vehicles using the system were put into service with the London and Vienna fire brigades. Porsche

Chapter 1

Ferdinand Porsche

New Thinking For a New Century

Ferdinand Porsche's life began in 1875, at the end of what historians call the Industrial Revolution, but he was destined to play a large role in another revolution: the dramatic shift from horse to horsepower. His mechanical creations would influence every aspect of twentieth century transportation, from tractors to airplanes, from the simplest automobiles for the masses to the most sophisticated racing machines for the nobility. Porsche's legacy would carry on for decades after his death.

He was born in Maffersdorf, Bohemia, in the Austro-Hungarian empire, which is today part of Czechoslovakia. The young Ferdinand showed a mechanical inclination from an early age. He was not an outstanding student in his early studies or at the Imperial Technical School in nearby Reichensberg, but his fascination with things electrical led to his building an electrical generating plant for the family home, at a time when many people in the region had never seen an electric light. Dismissing the young man's effort as a foolish waste of time, the senior Porsche angrily kicked away the acid-filled batteries, ruining his shoes but leaving his son's determination undiminished. Young Ferdinand's career would be marked by these two traits, possibly inherited: a determined spirit and a temper.

While his father, Anton, wanted the young man to join him as an apprentice in the family metal shop, Ferdinand was hardly excited by the prospect of spending his life as a tinsmith. The owner of a local factory offered to sponsor him in a move to Vienna where a job at an electrical equipment company was secured. Moving to Vienna at the age of eighteen, Ferdinand worked at Bela Egger for four years, first as a general laborer and later, when his talents became obvious, as a manager. During his first years away from home, he also sought to better educate himself, and though later in life a number of honorary titles would be bestowed upon him, his only formal higher education was during this time in Vienna and consisted of a brief period as a part-time, unregistered student at the *Technische Hochschule* (Technical University). One thinks of Vienna at the turn of the century as a romantic place, and it must have been for young Porsche; he fell in love with Aloisia Kaes, a girl in the office where he worked. They were married in Maffersdorf and their first child was a daughter, Louise.

Porsche's interest in the exciting new field of electricity, his working experience at Bela Egger and his technical studies paved the way for an offer of employment with Vienna coachbuilder Jacob Lohner. Lohner catered to the cream of Austrian society and was optimistic for the future of electric automobiles. The idea of quiet, smoke-free power would appeal to his blue-blood clientele, and Lohner saw the potential in this energetic young man who, he believed, could bring the idea to life. Porsche, by this time, had probably already formulated the basic concept for such a vehicle, and within two years had produced a unique design that used electric motors on the front wheel hubs. This eliminated the need for and the weight of the entire conventional drivetrain, but of the 2,150 lb. total weight, almost half was batteries and compared to gas-powered vehicles, the car could never be considered fast or long ranging. It did, however, create quite a stir at the Paris Exposition of 1900 where Porsche demonstrated it and won a grand prize. It was a marvel of ingenuity, and incidentally, the world's first practical front-wheel-drive car. Ferdinand Porsche was twenty-five years old.

The next step taken by the young designer was to become something of a pattern for later years. Not content with the performance of the electric-drive car, he lightened and modified it to enter a hillclimb at the Semmering Pass on September 23, 1900. He easily bested the previous record time for electric cars by more than fifty percent at the amazing average speed of 25 mph. This and other hillclimbs in the first decade of the new century began a tradition that would make the name of Porsche well known in racing circles for years to come.

Work continued on Lohner's electric carriages for the next few years. Further refinements included rear-drive and four-wheel-drive versions, and a hybrid with a gas engine and an electric engine dubbed Mixt in which the gas engine drove a generator for the electric motors. In a 1902 military exercise, Porsche was at the wheel of a Mixt-drive Mercedes-Lohner-Porsche and beside him was no less a personage than Archduke Franz Ferdinand of Austria. It was perhaps the first time—but certainly not the last—in which a Porsche design would place its creator center stage in the arena of national politics. Dressed on that day in the military uniform of a reserve infantryman, it is ironic that this man, who had no interest in politics and was anything but the military type, would soon be immersed in both.

In 1905, Porsche saw greener pastures in the direction of Austro-Daimler, Austria's largest and most prestigious car maker, a branch of the German Daimler company. He was hired as technical director, a position of importance for a thirty-year-old man, especially in light of the fact that he was replacing Paul Daimler, son of the founder, Gottlieb. Development of the Mixt-drive continued for a time, but by 1906, Porsche began work on conventional-drive automobiles.

Lohner had sold his patents that year to Austrian businessman Emil Jellinek, an entrepreneur and purveyor of fine automobiles to wealthy customers across the Continent. As a young man Jellinek had traveled the world and by the turn of the century had become interested in Gottlieb Daimler's motorcars. He was a catalyst in the development of "sports cars," something that heretofore existed only in the minds of certain automobile owners. He prodded the Stuttgart factory to build more powerful yet more refined cars and while doing so, made motoring a status sport among his affluent friends. The youngest Jellinek daughter had given her name, Mercedes, to the Daimler cars that her father raced and sold. Jellinek also sold many Austro-Daimlers, and another daughter's name was given to one of their four-cylinder machines, the Maja. It was this model, already part of the A-D line-up when he arrived, that Porsche developed into a sporting version with 32 hp and a four-speed gearbox to be entered at the Prince Henry Trials of 1909.

Sponsored by the kaiser's auto-enthusiast brother Heinrich, this multi-stage, week-long race covered more than a thousand miles, and although the A-D team made a good showing, they were beaten by Fritz Opel's group. Some three months later, on September 19, at the Semmering hillclimb and once again driving a modified Maja, Porsche not only took first prize in his class, but returned home to an even greater prize. A son had been born in his absence, Ferdinand Anton Ernst Porsche.

Determined to succeed in the next year's Prince Henry Trials, Porsche approached Daimler in Stuttgart about a mutual effort, but was refused any help. His response was to design an aerodynamic (for its day) four-seat touring car with an 86 hp, 5.7 liter ohc four-cylinder based on an aircraft engine. The design demonstrated his preference for efficiency rather than the brute size of some of the competition's 20.0 liter engines. With Porsche's cars capable of almost 90 mph, the A-D team was victorious in 1910. It was a one-two-three finish for Austro-Daimler, with the designer himself driving the winning car and his wife in the passenger seat.

Other projects undertaken during this time included aircraft engines of many types; one in particular could be considered an early ancestor of the VW. This unit was an air-cooled horizontally opposed four, somewhat in the shape of an X. Porsche also showed his versatility by designing units that were inline, V and W configurations and fighter plane engines of advanced design. The electric vehicle concepts were not forgotten, however, and as war clouds gathered on the

Prinz Heinrich Fahrt, Austria, 1910
Ferdinand Porsche at the wheel of an Austro-Daimler Tulpenwagen, so named for its tulip-shaped aerodynamic body. Porsche drove the winning car in a one-two-three sweep of the 1910 "Prinz Heinrich Fahrt." Porsche

horizon, heavy industries all across Europe geared up for an escalating arms race already under way by 1913. This was the year that Austro-Daimler took control of the armament firm Skoda, and the next year Archduke Franz Ferdinand, Porsche's one-time military parade passenger, was assassinated in Sarajevo, Yugoslavia, marking the beginning of the war to end all wars.

World War I Military Engineering

Skoda built the guns for the Imperial Austrian Army, and what guns they were! Porsche's responsibility was to move the artillery—no easy task when the unit in question was a 26 ton, 420 mm cannon that fired 1 ton shells. His solution was a monstrous road train called C Zug. Led by a Mixt generator-tractor, up to ten independently steered wagons with electric hub motors would follow. Hitched together and connected by electrical cables, they carried assorted cannon, shells and supplies, often over extremely difficult terrain. For this and other successful military design work Porsche received an honorary doctorate from the Vienna Technical University in 1916. In addition, he was awarded the order of Franz Josef, a high honor even though the empire itself was about to crumble.

As the great war drew to a close, Porsche was appointed managing director of Austro-Daimler and was soon faced with the challenge of keeping the company alive. Having geared up for production of war materiel, it was now necessary to completely redirect assembly operations for civilian products as soon as possible. The German and Austrian economies were a shambles, however, and few people were able to afford the large vehicles that had been the mainstay of Austro-Daimler before the war. Porsche believed that a small, efficient car was what the public needed but it would be three years before he was able to make any progress toward it.

Sascha: Development and Racing

The first postwar Grand Prix event took place in Brescia, Italy, in the summer of 1921. Attending the event were Dr. Porsche (as he was now known), his friend Count Alexander "Sascha" Kolowrat, a wealthy Austrian filmmaker, and eleven-year-old Ferdinand Anton Porsche, known as Ferry. The group was particularly impressed by the light and nimble Bugattis, and the Count provided incentive for Porsche to begin work on a similar car. With Kolowrat underwriting the development costs, Austro-Daimler agreed to allow limited production as a sports racer. By early the next year the design of the Sascha (named after Kolowrat) was complete: a four-cylinder overhead-cam engine of 1100 cc displacement that could power the lightweight body to almost 90 mph. Next came road tests, which involved a careful running in of the

engine, then a teardown, adjustment and more running in. One of the drivers entrusted with this critical task was Ferry Porsche who, even at the age of twelve, showed a definite penchant for the automotive world.

A group of four Saschas was entered in the 1922 Targa Florio road race. Standard cars placed first and second in the under 1100 cc class, and a young man named Alfred Neubauer—who would later gain fame as head of Mercedes-Benz racing—drove a 1500 cc version to sixth place in the racing car class against much more powerful cars. It was a triumph for Porsche and for Austro-Daimler, though the board of directors refused to build the car as a regular production model. The next year at Monza the A-D team, including young Ferry Porsche, watched as one of its drivers lost control and was killed in a high-speed accident during the race. When the board of directors then decided to discontinue racing, it was another wedge driven between them and their technical director who already had plans under way for a 2.0 liter successor to the Sascha. By 1922, Porsche and the board were at odds over larger issues involving the way the company was run. Not one to mince words or actions, he resigned and set his sights on bigger and better opportunities.

Porsche was hired as chief designer at Daimler in Stuttgart and began work early in 1923. The new job would entail a move from Wiener Neustadt, Austria, to Germany and the family, including Frau Porsche, daughter Louise and young Ferry, moved into a new house on the Fuerbacher Weg in Stuttgart in December of that year. Porsche was again filling a position vacated by Paul Daimler who had recently left the company. Part of the new arrangement was a seat on the board for Porsche, giving him more control over management decisions. Karl Rabe, who would later figure prominently in the Porsche design organization, replaced him at Austro-Daimler.

The Mercedes-Benz Years

When Ferdinand Porsche came to *Daimler Moteren Gesellschaft,* he inherited a tradition of racing successes that stretched back before the turn of the century. During the war, great strides were made in aero engine development while automobile production came to a standstill. Paul Daimler had done much work on supercharging, an infant technology of force feeding air to an engine to extract more power from a given displacement and a means of overcoming the effects of thin air at high altitudes. By the time peacetime racing resumed on the Continent, Daimler and company were experts in the field and immediately set about applying the technology to automobiles and racing.

Porsche's initial work with Daimler was to develop their small 1.5 and 2.0 liter four-cylinder cars. The 2.0 liter racing machines were already on their way to Indianapolis when Porsche took over in 1923, and even though they suffered spectacular mechanical failures at the Brickyard (due to improper boost and valve timing), the American public got their first look at supercharged racing cars. Within a year the distinctive scream of compressor engines would be heard on racecourses across America and Europe. Subsequent changes to the Indianapolis Daimler made by Porsche transformed the racer: the compression ratio was lowered from 7.5:1 to 4.5:1, a larger, slower-turning Roots blower was built and the exhaust

valves were filled with mercury for better cooling. In this improved model, Christian Werner won the Targa Florio in April 1924. Again Porsche proved the worth of a small, highly efficient machine.

When Porsche first took up his duties at Daimler, German officials informed him that his honorary doctorate from the Vienna Technical University was not valid in Germany and that he must not use the title while in that country. Yet only a year later the same title was conferred upon him by the Stuttgart Technische Hochschule for his work in bringing glory to

Targa Florio, Sicily, 1924
The name Porsche was to become well known at the Sicilian Targa Florio race. In this supercharged Daimler, Christian Werner won the

1924 race and earned Porsche, center, his second honorary Doctorate. Porsche

14

Daimler at the 1924 Targa Florio. It was his first great success at Daimler.

Porsche was prodigious, working at the same time on another 2.0 liter of an extremely advanced design for the day, with crankshaft roller bearings, dry-sump lubrication, two overhead cams and four valves per cylinder. It could run to 6000 rpm and made 160 hp with supercharger, but by the time it was fully developed the 1926 Grand Prix formula of 1.5 liters had rendered it obsolete.

Also in development at the time was a car that was anything but small. Daimler had a tradition of *Hoechsleistung Tourenwagens*, or high-performance touring cars and by 1925, two new six-cylinder engines, designed by Porsche from the start to be supercharged, were on the market. The larger of these, the 6.2 liter 24/100/140 (the numbers respectively referred to taxable horsepower, actual horsepower and horsepower with supercharger engaged) was the basis for a series of cars destined to become legendary. It was a light aluminum-alloy block with cylinder barrels and head of cast iron. Valves were operated by a vertical shaft driving spur gears to the overhead cam. A Roots blower was installed at the front of the engine and like all previous Mercedes supercharged cars, pushing the accelerator pedal past a stop to the floor engaged the blower and changed the vehicle from a torquey, placid workhorse to a galloping charger.

Unfortunately, the first chassis that were mated to the new engines were grand tourers indeed. These dreadnoughts of the fleet were often so ponderous as to completely cancel out the high-performance part of the equation. But in 1926, a new model appeared called the K for Kurz, or shortened wheelbase. Fitted with a variety of sporting bodies, the new cars were well received by wealthy sportsmen. Porsche's original intentions for the machine were fulfilled when in 1927, the 36/120/180, or S model, appeared with an engine now enlarged to 6.8 liters and the frame arched over the rear wheels to provide a lower center of gravity. Following in the next three years were the SS of 7.1 liters and 225 hp, SSK and a final variation on the theme, the SSKL with a drilled frame for lightness and a top speed of more than 150 mph.

In 1927, the inaugural event at the new Nürburgring was won by Rudolf Caracciola in a Mercedes-Benz S against more nimble competition. New Formula Libre rules the next year allowed a wide variety of engine sizes, and the new SS continued to win, even though its size and weight often put it at a disadvantage. The mechanical drum brakes were at best marginally effective, but Porsche's engine could accelerate the beast from 5 to 105 mph in top gear without strain, and the cars literally roared past everything in sight.

These great white sharks of the open road were a long way from the car for the masses that Porsche still envisioned, however. In its final form, the SSKL chassis alone sold for $13,550 without bodywork. Porsche seemed to be a man who could not decline a challenging problem, especially if it involved racing, and the S series were just a few of sixty-five projects that he worked on during only five years at Daimler. The 1926 merger with Benz brought a shakeup to the car and truck lines, and also to the staffs of both companies. Hans Nibel, the chief designer at Benz, was more of a suspension expert than an engine man like Porsche. They shared duties for two years after the merger, but the line of medium-sized cars offered by the company at that time was dull but dependable, and one can assume that Porsche was anxious for greater challenges. He resigned in a huff after the 2.6 liter Stuttgart tourer ran into teething problems late in 1928.

The Year at Steyr

In 1929, the Porsche family was again on the move, as Dr. and Frau Porsche took up residence in Austria where he began work with Steyr as chief engineer and technical director. The Stuttgart villa was rented to Dr. Nibel. Young Ferry, who had completed an apprenticeship at the Robert Bosch company in Stuttgart, went on to study in Vienna at the *Technische Hochschule* at the insistence of his father. He stayed with his older sister Louise, who had married Viennese lawyer Anton Piëch.

Porsche's tenure at Steyr was only a year long, but during that time he developed a 2.0 liter six that was similar to the Stuttgart from Mercedes, but featuring an overhead cam and independent suspension. The big brother to this model was a 5.3 liter eight that would transport five in comfort. Porsche drove it to the Paris Auto Salon, the oldest and most prestigious automobile show at the time. Porsche's habit was to visit the exhibition each year where he studied the competition and talked shop with his peers. The 1929 show was a triumph for him, as his eight-cylinder Austria model enjoyed favorable reviews. On his return, he found that the Viennese bank that was a major Steyr shareholder had failed. The company was taken over by Austro-Daimler's bank, and working for A-D once again was not appealing to Porsche. He resigned and made plans to return to Stuttgart.

Chapter 2

Porsche Design Bureau

Independence: From the Heights to the Depths

At age fifty-five, Ferdinand Porsche took a hard look at his prospects. His reputation as an automotive designer was known around the world, as was his reputation as a difficult employee. Following his departure from Daimler-Benz, he received offers from Skoda and General Motors, but decided to proceed with a plan he had been considering for many years: to open his own design firm. The demand for his services was by no means ensured, however. The Depression that had struck America was also being felt across Europe and

Ernst von Delius at the wheel of the Porsche-designed Auto Union P-Wagen grand prix racer in 1936. The car was centered around its midships-mounted V-16 engine, which initially displaced 4.3 liters. The rear axle was originally mounted on transverse leaf springs, but was later changed to torsion bars fitted inside of the frame. The P in the model's name stood for Porsche. Porsche

many German car makers were on shaky ground. In fishing for new business, he planned to cast his net far and wide, as stated in the official title of the new firm, *Dr.-Ing. h.c. F. Porsche G.m.b.H., Konstruktionsbüro für Motoren, Fahrzeug, Luftfahrzeug, und Wasserfahrzeugbau.* This appellation as designers of motors, automobiles, airplanes and ships, lofty as it was, would prove appropriate in a few years.

Stuttgart was already a center of industry for the automobile, and it was decided to locate the design office there. Although Dr. Hans Nibel still rented the family villa in Stuttgart, the family moved back to the city in temporary quarters. The matter of financing and running the business operations of a new company was not so easily resolved for Dr. Porsche, who was admittedly not an expert in the fine points of commerce. He looked to Adolph Rosenberger, a wealthy former racer from nearby Pforzheim, Germany, who had a keen interest in automobiles as well as a thorough knowledge of business. Rosenberger agreed to invest in the new venture and come aboard as business manager.

Porsche next set about the job of building a staff, and here he showed a talent that almost equaled his mechanical genius. Though he was often an irascible character, he was able to inspire others to produce their best work. The first member of the new Design Bureau was senior engineer Karl Rabe, who had carried on at Austro-Daimler after Porsche's departure. Joining him were transmission specialist Karl Frohlich, engine man Josef Kales, and Josef Zahradnick who oversaw chassis and steering work. Porsche's nephew Ghislaine Kaes, with Josef Goldinger and Franz Sieberer were, respectively, Dr. Porsche's secretary, chief driver and blueprint technician. The original staff was joined soon afterward by body designer Erwin Komenda, who would pen the original 356 shape, Franz X. Reimspiess from Austro-Daimler and Josef Mickl, who was responsible for the involved calculations required for the aerodynamic engineering done by the firm. Most of this group were fellow Austrians in their early thirties, all former associates and loyal admirers of Dr. Porsche. They came from a number of different companies, and surely none of them signed on with a get-rich-quick attitude. Porsche's son-in-law Dr. Anton Piëch also became a key member of the original staff along with Ferry Porsche, who left the Vienna Technical University to continue his education in a hands-on manner with his father's new firm.

The new concern opened its doors in December 1930, at 14 Kronenstrasse in Stuttgart. Yet even before this official start, a contract with the Wanderer company was signed. Porsche believed the most logical way to keep track of each new commission was with a sequential numbering system. His staff

The big brother to the Porsche Design Bureau's first project, the graceful Type 8 Wanderer prototype, which became Ferdinand Porsche's personal car. Porsche

agreed, but admonished him to begin with the number seven. The general feeling was that the firm must not look as though it was starting from scratch. This initial project number seven was a small six-cylinder sedan of 1.7 to 2.0 liter displacement that proved quite popular. The management of Wanderer was pleased and requested a larger touring car. Porsche responded by designing an elegantly streamlined two-door with a 3.2 liter eight. Plans called for a supercharger, but before the car was complete, Wanderer became a victim of the economic times. The company was merged with Horch, Audi and DKW to form Auto Union, whose four-circle logo carries on to this day in the Audi line. The beautiful Project 8 did not go to waste, however. Dr. Porsche used it as his personal car for four more years. It's just as well that Porsche didn't have to buy a new car, as he may not have been able to afford one. The tenuous financial footing of the company did not improve during the next two years and the staff often had to accept salary in installments.

Predecessors to the People's Car

In December 1931, the firm was approached by the owner of Zündapp motorcycles, Herr Neumeyer, who wanted to produce, in his words, a "Volksauto" to take up slack in his factory while demand for motorcycles was low. Neumeyer's designers had no experience with automobiles, so he consulted Porsche, who already had design studies for this type of car. A "people's car" was a dream of Porsche's that his various employers had never shared, but it now seemed to have a chance of fulfillment. As new customers had not been standing in line at 14 Kronenstrasse, Porsche had taken the available time to lay out some of the basic elements for his small, efficient auto, and by the time he met Neumeyer, much of the design that would become the Volkswagen—and later, the Porsche—was already on paper.

The staff went to work with enthusiasm, and Neumeyer, for his part, was not overly concerned about particulars. Cheap, simple and easy to produce in his own factory were his main concerns. A four-cylinder boxer engine was considered, but the three prototypes that were built had five-cylinder water-cooled radial engines mounted in the rear, slightly inclined from the vertical to follow the rear roofline. There are other design features that show this Project 12 to be a genesis of the VW: aerodynamic body with rear engine and mid gearbox, but a more likely basis for the people's car was soon to arrive. A series of mechanical problems with the Zündapp prototypes and the cost of manufacturing his own engines soon caused Neumeyer to have second thoughts about the whole project. When the sales of motorcycles took an upward swing in 1933, he decided to cancel the project, paid Porsche for the developmental work and walked away from an auto-

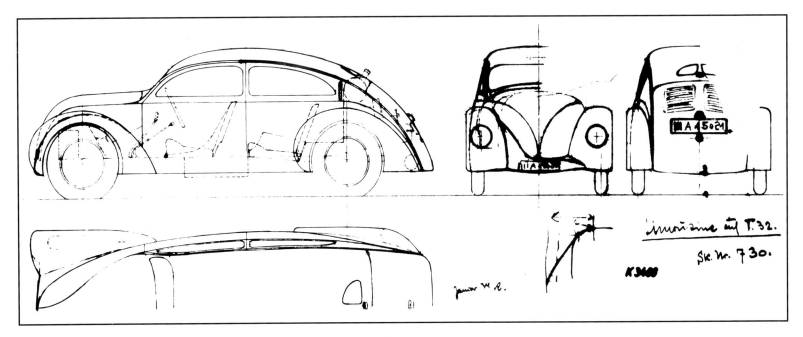

The NSU Type 32 prototype built by Reutter gave an indication of greater things to come in both shape and layout. Porsche

motive market that would prove to be larger than he ever imagined.

Still anxious for new business, the fledgling company accepted a commission from the NSU motorcycle company in Neckarsulm, Germany, whose director, Fritz von Falkenhayn, had great admiration for Dr. Porsche, and more importantly, would not meddle in the design of a new small car. This latest project, Type 32, was much closer to the Volkswagen. One interesting feature was the new torsion bar suspension; Porsche applied for a patent but was informed that some twenty-year-old theoretical drawings existed from France. This vaguely similar French design had been awarded a patent even though no actual suspension of this type had been built.

The new Type 32 was slightly larger in size and engine capacity than the Volkswagen would be, but its other features made it a true precursor of the most popular car in history. A 1.5 liter engine was fitted behind the transmission, the latest in a long line of Porsche-designed air-cooled engines. His engines were used in airplanes, gun carriages and trains as early as 1912, and Porsche had a firm belief in air cooling as the best solution for an all-purpose powerplant. The NSU prototypes were built as a series of three, two by coachbuilder Drauz in Heibronn, using a wooden frame covered with artificial leather and one in metal by Reutter, located near the Porsche offices in Stuttgart. Like the Zündapp prototypes, these were built in secrecy at night, and like Zündapp, NSU motorcycle sales took off in 1933. Fiat, which had an interest in the NSU company, got wind of the plan and let von Falkenhayn know that they would take legal action to prevent what they considered competition to their own small cars. NSU was forced to pay off Porsche and cancel the project. Having taken two distinct steps toward the people's car, it now appeared to Porsche that the concept might go no further.

A mysterious interlude took place in early 1932 when Dr. Porsche was approached by a man who said he represented the Soviet government. Karl Rabe and others thought the subject might be a tractor commission, but in a subsequent meeting, the Russian emissary proposed that Porsche come to Russia and tour its centers of industry. It was an unusual proposition, since there existed almost no exchange of technology between Germany and Russia—indeed, the political climate had been cool for some time. Porsche, assuming the chance of a consulting contract or purchase of his patent rights, agreed to go. During a lengthy trip he was given a grand tour of Russian foundries, factories and engineering centers and a rare insight into the state of its technology. While he enjoyed the status of an honored guest of state, weeks passed before the Soviets finally made a startling announcement: they would like Dr. Porsche to become State Designer of Rus-

sia. The offer was enticing, and Porsche was more than a bit flattered, but even beyond the language barrier was the thought that a man almost sixty years old would find it difficult to uproot his family and start a new life in a strange country. He would have ample opportunity to build the "people's tractor" in Russia, but two other projects close to his heart, a people's car and a state-of-the-art racing machine, were not part of the Soviet agenda. Porsche returned to Stuttgart to continue building the new company—after all, it was *his* name on the door.

Government-Sponsored Prosperity

The early years of the Porsche Design Bureau were lean times, indeed, and new commissions came less frequently than the men had hoped. But the fortunes of the company were soon to change, and one man in particular was responsible for Porsche's success in the 1930s: a mustachioed fellow Austrian with a keen interest in automobiles. On January 30, 1933, Adolf Hitler became chancellor of Germany, and his effect on the German automobile industry was quickly felt. At the opening of the 1933 Berlin Auto Show, the new chancellor startled the crowd by announcing that there would be no more taxes on cars or motorcycles, and that he planned to build a network of fast, smooth superhighways—autobahns—across the country. In addition, the German government would subsidize the building of Grand Prix cars. His intention was to show German superiority through technology: the master race as master racers, and the well-attended Grand Prix races were the perfect venues for such an exercise of self-aggrandizement.

At the time, it was assumed by almost everyone that the government's 500,000 marks earmarked for the development of these new cars would go to Daimler-Benz, whose size and resources could certainly produce the machine needed to bring glory to the Third Reich. One of the few people who thought otherwise was Ferdinand Porsche, who, with his staff, had previously spent many months drawing up plans for just such a vehicle. The original idea came to Porsche after the International Sports Commission (AIACR) in Paris decided in October 1932 that their new formula would set a weight limit of 750 kg dry (1,657 lb.), but with virtually no other constraints. Porsche was thrilled: here was a clean sheet of paper on which he could pursue his dream of a race car the likes of which the world had never seen.

Adolph Rosenberger was an enthusiastic promoter of the idea. Rosenberger had raced a "teardrop" Benz car in the mid 1920s, and the new Porsche design would bear a striking resemblance to this earlier mid-engine vehicle. With few other paying customers at the time, and with Rosenberger willing to finance the project, by mid-November 1932, Karl Rabe had written a calculation sheet that outlined the new car's specifications, including a V–16 engine of 4358 cc with the potential for 182 mph.

A new company, separate from the Porsche Design Bureau, was formed to build and perhaps even campaign the cars in the future—Hochleistungs-Fahrzeug-Bau GmbH (High Performance Vehicle Construction Company, Inc.). Also planned, though never built, was a 4.4 liter V–16, 200 hp sports car capable of 125 mph, Porsche Type 52. While the blueprints for

the race car were being created, conversations took place between Porsche and Auto Union, which was shopping around for an image-builder for the new company. Auto Union was willing to build the racer, but understandably, wanted a piece of Hitler's subsidy for the project.

Hans Stuck was a racing driver with experience in Porsche's creations for both Austro-Daimler and Mercedes, and a great talent for knowing the right people. One of his connections was the new *Reichskanzler*, who early in 1933

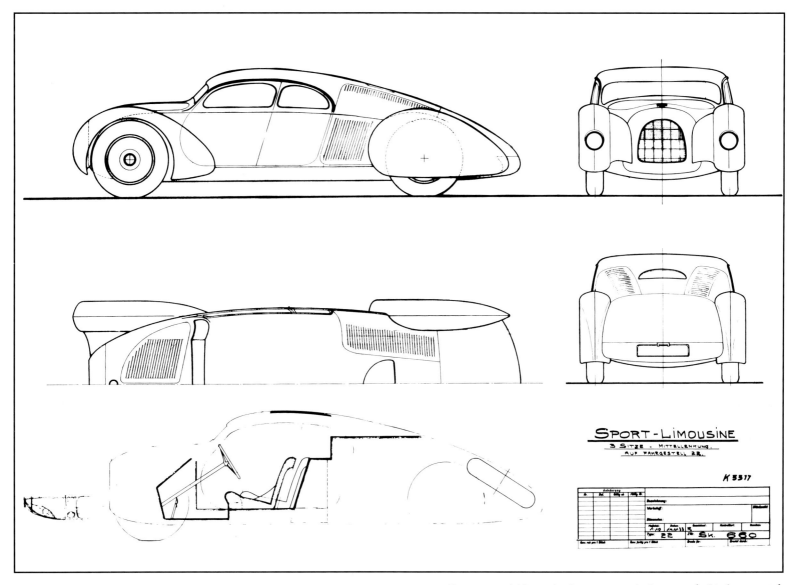

The Type 52 was a "street version" of Porsche's Auto Union grand prix car. With a mid-engine V-16 tuned to 200 hp, the three-place, 2,860 lb. car would have had a top speed of 125 mph. Unfortunately for enthusiasts of the day, it was never built. Porsche kept a two-year-old promise to find Stuck a car to race. Stuck was surprised that Hitler had remembered, and he quickly went to see Ferdinand Porsche. On May 10, a meeting took place in Berlin with the Führer during which Dr. Porsche suggested that a bit of competition between manufacturers might be healthy. He went on to explain that his new design was complete, and Auto Union was ready to build it. Hitler, swayed not only by Porsche's arguments but by his respect for the man, agreed to split the money evenly between Auto Union and Mercedes. The new contract for Porsche brought part of Auto Union's subsidy money back to Stuttgart, and development work began. The initial prototype, with a 4.3 liter supercharged V–16 engine, produced almost 250 hp at 4500 rpm and later versions would be 6.0 liters and more than 500 hp. Ready by late fall, its first test driver was Ferry Porsche, who in his book, *We at Porsche,* describes the sensation: "when you finally got a decent road grip, you could then kick down the throttle, get a howling, almost deafening response from the engine and absolutely catapult down the road. There is no other word for it." Ferry's career as a race driver was short-lived, however. His father sensed his talent behind the wheel, but saw an even greater talent at the drawing board and explained, "I have enough drivers, but only one son!"

The P-wagen, as it was known, made its debut at the Berlin Avus track in March 1934 with Stuck at the wheel. In this first outing, Stuck set records for 100 and 200 kilometers and for average speed—134.9 mph. A poster proclaiming "Three World Records for Germany" took quick advantage of the propaganda and advertising value of the run. During its first race on May 27, 1934, again at Avus, August Momberger placed third behind two Alfa Romeos and it was not until its fourth event, the German Grand Prix, that the car won the first of three victories for that year.

The new Daimler-Benz W25, designed by Hans Nibel, took to the tracks shortly after the Auto Union team and began a two-way duel for Grand Prix supremacy that lasted until war came in 1939. In 1935, the Mercedes Silver Arrows took most of the race honors, but the tables were turned the next year. The Porsche approach, using a mid-engine layout with torsion bar suspension, gave rise to a reputation for quirky handling and indeed, few drivers ever mastered the beast. But other innovations like center-mounted saddle tanks kept the car balanced in spite of fuel level. The Auto Union cars garnered more than their share of attention wherever they appeared, mainly due to the unusual layout, and at races Ferdinand Porsche was often on hand to oversee the operation and lend advice.

The Auto Union racers were built at Horch's Zwichau plant and Porsche persuaded Prof. Robert Eberan von Eber-horst, an automotive engineer at Dresden University, to join AU and oversee the project. Hans Stuck was joined on the Auto Union team by such other notable drivers as Achille Varzi, Bernd Rosemeyer and Tazio Nuvolari (in 1938). In six seasons, Mercedes and AU competed together on forty-seven occasions, and of these, only one race was not won by either of the two. The 1938 formula called for 3.0 liter engines, but Porsche's contract with Auto Union had already expired and he was free to pursue another tantalizing goal—the absolute land speed record.

The Reich, the Records and Rosemeyer

German races had the structure of carefully orchestrated political rallies, under the direction of the ONS, the governing body of German motorsport. Adolf Hühnlein, a dour army functionary, was *Korpsführer* of the ONS and the NSKK, the national driver's corps. In addition to being master of ceremonies to stiff-armed crowds of military types, he was responsible for organizing speed contests and was able to marshal thousands of troops to close off the autobahns during record runs. By the spring of 1935 the endeavor had become a game of one-upmanship between the two German teams and speed marks were changing hands weekly. Even Tazio Nuvolari went record chasing in an Alfa Romeo.

By record week in October 1937, Auto Union's Bernd Rosemeyer became the first man to exceed 250 mph on the road. Rudolf Caracciola in a Mercedes soon bettered this achievement with runs at 266 mph on a January morning near Frankfurt. Caracciola described driving at those speeds on the

Auto Union's P-Wagen brought the name Porsche to the attention of racing fans the world over. Unusual in its day, the mid-engine design, like so many other Porsche innovations, would become the norm in later years. Porsche

narrow autobahn: "the road constricted to a narrow white band with overpasses that seemed like small, black holes...." That same afternoon, Rosemeyer and the AU team arrived to avenge their honor. There was concern because the wind had picked up, but Rosemeyer insisted on proceeding with the plan. Near the end of his run a burst of wind from the side blew his car off course when he was traveling at more than 260 mph. He flew into a clump of trees, where he was found amid the wreckage. He died within a few minutes. With the loss of this most popular German driver, record breaking lost some of its luster, but early in 1939 Mercedes was back in the business, setting 3.0 liter speed marks.

Between Grand Prix races, both Mercedes and Auto Union had taken their cars to the vacant tracks and new autobahns, and a number of class and distance records now belonged to Germany. But the English had owned the absolute speed mark since 1929 and that really stuck in the Nazis' collective craw. In pursuit of this grail, Hans Stuck was once again instrumental in arranging for various players to combine resources. His idea intrigued Dr. Porsche and a new project, Type 80, an aerodynamic six-wheeled monster, took shape on the drawing board early in 1937. The vehicle would

The T-80 was intended to bring the world's land speed record to Germany, with its fighter-plane engine (not installed here) and an aerodynamic body. War came and it never turned a wheel under its own power. Porsche

be built by Daimler-Benz from Porsche's blueprints using their own newly developed inverted V–12 aircraft engine. Initially producing upwards of 800 hp, the DB 600 engine had the potential for almost 3,000 hp. The technical challenge was incentive for Stuck and Porsche; Mercedes-Benz would profit from the promotional exposure. But to the government, this was a matter of pride, and there was no question of taking the car to the Bonneville Salt Flats in Utah. The record attempt must be made on German highways, no matter how unsuitable for a 300 mph car.

The T–80 suffered numerous delays and the absolute speed record became a moving target; by 1939 it was almost 370 mph. Finally, late that year, a DB 603 V–12 engine of 44.5 liters and the potential for 3,000 hp was installed in the vehicle and preparations were made for record week 1940. It never came due to the war, and the T–80 never moved under its own power. Any regrets about the fate of the project were not in the fore of Dr. Porsche's thoughts, however. The design office in Stuttgart was now well into a project of more prosaic, but eminently practical purpose.

The People's Car

On his soapbox at the 1933 Berlin Auto Show, Adolf Hitler made a suggestion to the German auto manufacturers that they build a simple car that anyone could afford. The people took this as a promise, and the car makers as an order. Mercedes-Benz was already selling its 130 model with an air-cooled rear engine and shape similar to that of the Zündapp and NSU prototypes developed by Porsche. The 130 design, not surprisingly, dated from Porsche's tenure with Daimler-Benz but neither that company nor the other German manufacturers were enthusiastic about small, economical cars. There was not much money to be made with them, and when Hitler announced that he wanted the new car to sell for less than 1,000 marks, any factory interest disappeared.

Jacob Werlin, who was on the board of Daimler-Benz and was Hitler's advisor in things automotive, brought Porsche together with the chancellor in the fall of 1933 and the doctor presented a proposal for a people's car, or *volks wagen*, in the spring of 1934. Porsche's estimates called for a minimum selling price of 1,550 marks, more than half again what Hitler required. Had this been simply a car, it could never have been built, but it was a political contrivance and as such, it began to take shape on Porsche's drawing boards, ostensibly under the direction of ADAC, the Society of German Automobile Manufacturers.

The government contract called for 20,000 marks a month for the ten months it should take to construct prototypes. It was not much money and not much time, but the basics of the new vehicle were in the Zündapp and NSU prototypes, the latter only recently canceled. With this foundation already laid, Porsche's staff was able to design and assemble three prototypes, VW 3, by February 1936 in the garage of the family home at Fuerbacher Weg. These units were thoroughly tested until Christmas of that year and a report was then written by ADAC recommending further development of the model. Ferry Porsche was by now involved in testing and trouble-shooting on the project, but took a short holiday after his marriage to Dorothea Reitz in January 1935. Their first son, Ferdinand Alexander, was born the following December.

In 1937, Daimler-Benz built thirty improved experimental cars, VW 30, that were test driven more than a million miles, day and night, by Hühnlein's NSKK troops. By 1938, a final batch of test and demonstrator cars, in near-final form as VW

38, was built to promote the new venture, which by now transcended being just an automobile. For his part in the glorious endeavor, Ferdinand Porsche was awarded the German national prize, worth 100,000 marks.

A parallel development was taking place in the agricultural field, which Hitler felt was in need of mechanization. He wanted farmers to have tractors and the Porsche Design Bureau complied with three versions of a small, all-purpose diesel machine, Types 110, 111 and 113. The idea was certainly not new to the doctor; his notebooks dating back to 1927 carried various specifications and ideas. But the Führer's orders put the project on the front burner and by 1938 the first of these tractor prototypes was built. Also in parallel with the VW, a new factory and city were to be built for production of the tractors at Waldbröl, but the plans went by the wayside

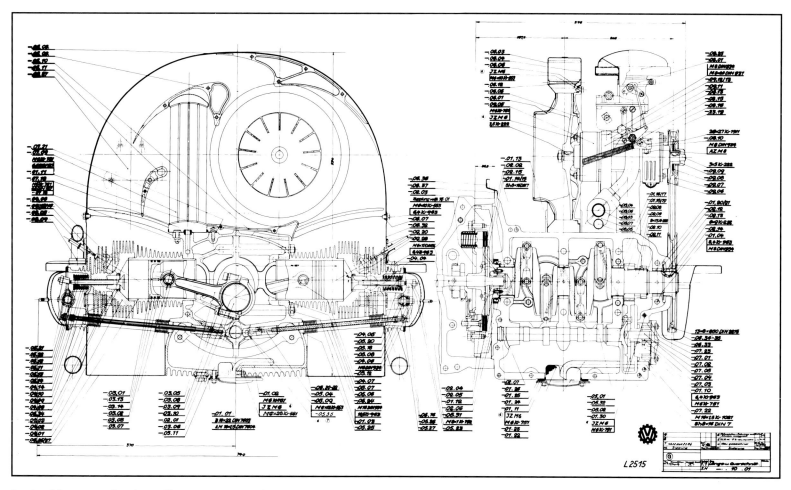

Design blueprints for the Volkswagen engine that would later power the first Porsche sports cars. Porsche

during hostilities. The project was resurrected immediately afterward and the postwar tractor versions were quite successful, but Waldbröl never became a household word like the town where Volkswagens were built.

On May 26, 1938, top-hatted masons in white coats laid the cornerstone for the new VW factory near Wolfsburg, a swampy middle-of-nowhere town in lower Saxony. Among the 70,000 present were Ferdinand and Ferry Porsche, both of whom had spent part of the previous summer in the United States studying mass-production methods and recruiting German-descended engineers to work in the new plant. After the inevitable speech, Hitler was driven to the train station at Fallersleben by Ferry Porsche in a VW convertible, one of three cars on display for the benefit of the *volk*. At the ceremony with Hitler was Robert Ley, whose *Kraft durch Freude*, or "Strength through Joy," branch of the party now controlled the manufacture and distribution method for the car: customers bought stamps and pasted them in a book to save for a car. When your 990 marks were paid, you got a car—supposedly. None of the 337,000 stamp collectors ever took delivery and only 630 KdF wagens were built for the government before production switched to military vehicles in 1940.

At the Porsche studio, the idea of building a competition version of the VW seemed plausible and sketches of an aluminum-bodied 1.5 liter sports car, Type 64, were drawn. But there was no enthusiasm from the state, which ran the

In front of the Porsche villa on the Feuerbacher Weg, one of the series VW 30, left, and an earlier version. By mid 1938, a final shape had evolved that excluded the "suicide" doors. This design cue had come from a visit to America where the Porsches, father and son, had found that American women preferred the more modest egress afforded by a front-hinged door. Porsche

entire VW enterprise, and it considered such ideas frivolous. The government managers would not supply components to Porsche to build their own sporting VW, so the concept of a sports car of their own—designed and built by Porsche—was revived by Ferdinand and Ferry Porsche in 1937. The company had prospered from the government contracts that now filled the drawing boards, and Karl Frohlich was able to devote enough time during 1938 to develop drawings for Type 114, a truly exotic sports car for the time. A mid-engine V-10 with double overhead shaft-driven cams, roller bearing crank and a five-speed transaxle were the main ingredients of this two-place streamliner, but actual construction would have to wait until the political situation calmed. Type 114 never saw the light of day, but its body shape emerged in another vehicle built to a specific purpose.

A race between Berlin and Rome, meant to propagandize their alliance and promote a new highway connecting the cities, was scheduled for September 1939. Since this event was state-sponsored, Porsche was able to procure parts and build a light, streamlined racer based on the lowly Volkswagen. The result was the Type 60K10—a narrow aluminum bodied car with a tuned 1500 cc engine capable of more than 90 mph. Erwin Komenda used the Type 114 shape as a basis but retained enough VW similarities to ensure that KdF customers could identify with the sleek racer. Bodies were made by Karosserie Rupflin in Munich and three cars were assembled in the garage facilities at the new Porsche offices at 2 Spitwaldstrasse in Zuffenhausen. Though the blitzkreig in Poland precluded the race, the cars were put to use as rapid transit for the company during the war, and only one survives to this day.

World War II Military Engineering

Dr. Porsche had been appointed one of the directors of the Volkswagen organization and spent much of his time at Wolfsburg during the war years. His son-in-law, Anton Piëch, became commercial director and general manager of the VW works, and the two men shared a small house on the outskirts of Wolfsburg when working there. For his work on the VW, in 1940 Dr. Porsche was given an honorary professorship by the minister for science and education. He was also appointed head of the Tank Commission by Dr. Fritz Todt. Porsche, now sixty-five, must have felt deep disappointment at seeing his people's car derailed by military needs. But the war brought an ever-increasing number of commissions to his design bureau including tanks and several versions of the VW military car, the *Kübelwagen* or "bucket car," Type 62 and later Type 82.

The Military Ordinance Office requested a military cross-country vehicle in 1939, and the VW chassis was adapted to this purpose with a utilitarian body. It quickly proved its worth in North Africa and on the Russian front. When the Allies invaded Europe, even they preferred captured Kübelwagens to their own Jeeps. Some 60,000 of these units were built as well as another 14,000 amphibious versions called the *Schwimmwagen*, Type 128 and Type 166, a smaller unit for the SS. Variations on the theme included half-track, four-wheel-drive and ski-mounted versions.

In designing tanks for the army, Porsche engineers used the Mixt-drive system that he had pioneered at the turn of the century, usually with a diesel engine. Their first, the Type 100 Leopard from the late 1930s, had two V-10 engines each displacing 10.0 liters and producing 210 hp, but the tank was

never series produced. A new version was designed and prototypes built for government approval: the Type 101 Tiger weighed in at 59 tons using two 15.0 liter engines with or without electric drive and using either gearbox or hydraulic drive by the Voith company. Albert Speer, the new armaments minister, awarded the contract to another company but the Type 101 was renamed Ferdinand and 100 were put to use as tank destroyers with a long-range 5 in. cannon. Another tank project, undertaken on orders from Hitler in 1942, was meant to be a "land battleship." This mobile pillbox, Type 205, was put on paper by December 1942, but a year passed before the prototype was ready for testing. At 188 tons, it was doubted by some that the vehicle could turn at all, but at its first

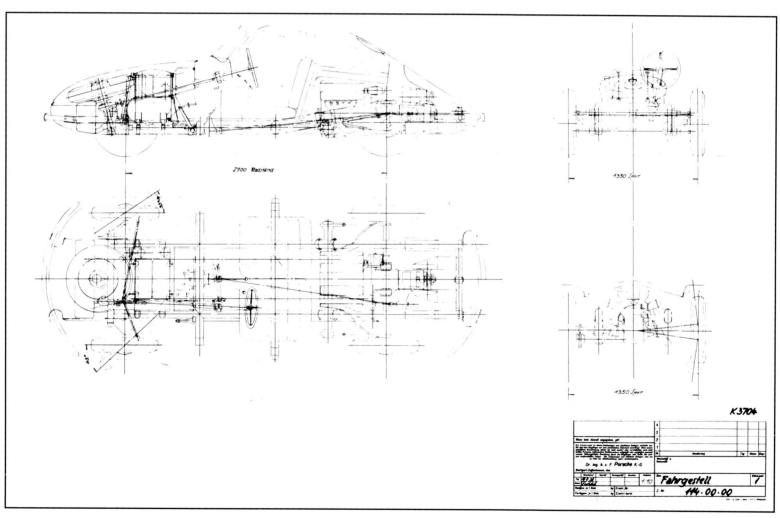

Design blueprint for the Porsche Type 114, which was to have an oval-tube ladder frame carrying two passengers and the midships-

mounted V-10 engine. The Type 114 was planned as a production car, but unfortunately it never made it to the assembly lines. Porsche

demonstration, it was able to swivel completely around well within its own length, 33.8 ft. Two of these monsters, dubbed *Maus*, or "Mouse," were constructed, though they never saw action and at war's end became just more monuments to Hitler's misplaced priorities.

The Stuttgart offices were filled with designs and plans for a variety of wartime projects including generating plants, tracked personnel carriers and even a supercharged VW engine, meant to be used in a stationary, high-altitude application. It was tested extensively in Ferry Porsche's personal

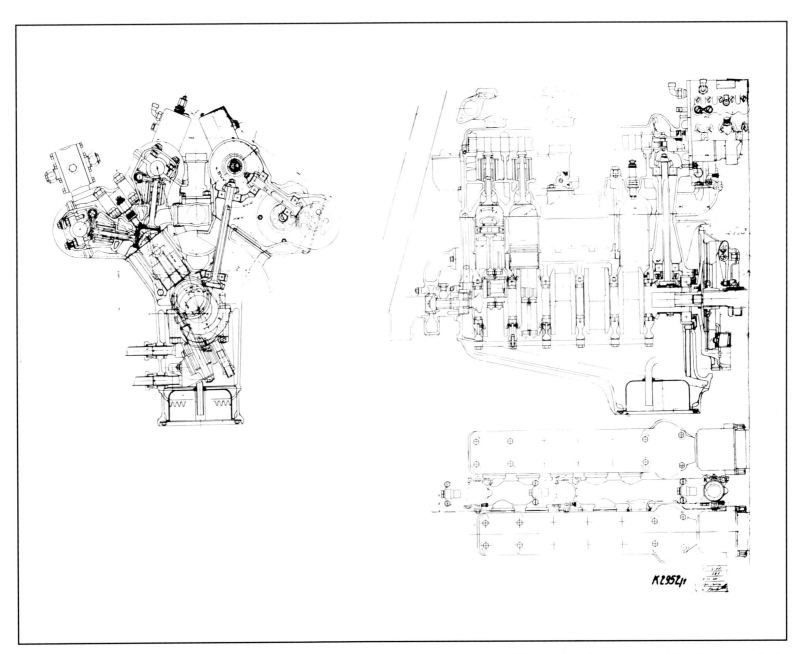

The Porsche Type 114 would have carried a V–10 engine with shaft-driven double-overhead-cams mounted amidships. A similar valve arrangement would be used in the Carrera and Spyder engines in the fifties. Porsche

Volkswagen and its 45 hp allowed him to get from one place to another quickly—a real benefit in dodging the ever-increasing bomber attacks.

By early 1944, it was recognized not only by the Porsches but by the government as well that Stuttgart was not a safe haven for the talent concentrated at the Porsche headquarters. Orders were given to move the company, and Ferry Porsche took up the job of finding a suitable location. Sensing that a move east was not in their best interest, two locations to the south were settled upon. One, a small flying school at Zell-am-See in Austria, adjoined the Porsche summer estate there and was put to use mainly for storage of machine tools and duplicate documents. The assets of the Porsche firm were divided into three roughly equal parts: at Stuttgart, Zell-am-See and a former sawmill in the tiny Austrian village of Gmünd, where the remaining staff took up what work remained in the closing days of the war.

Porsche Imprisoned

At the end of the war in May 1945, the Porsche family was gathered at the Zell-am-See estate where they were visited by Allied military representatives. Zell was in the American zone, and US intelligence officers were interested in Porsche's drawings and documents, so an army contingent was billeted at the flying school to ensure security. The soldiers found little excitement at the rural airstrip, so they made their own by racing the Berlin-Rome coupe stored there on the runway. As the height of summer approached, they turned it into a roadster with a metal shears. But their fun lasted only as long as the oil in the crankcase and the car soon ended up on the scrap pile.

Late in July, military police arrested Ferry Porsche and other company principals at the family estate on curious charges relating to a murder in Wolfsburg. Though innocent, they were held for months, interrogated about their wartime activities and finally released in November. Professor Porsche was at Gmünd in the British occupation zone that summer when he was arrested and taken to Kransberg castle where the Allies were determining which people should be tried as war criminals. He spent his seventieth birthday in confinement but was soon released and cleared of any suspicion, at least by the Americans. In mid-November both Ferry Porsche and his

Built for the Rome-Berlin race that was to take place in 1939, the shape of the Type 60K10 was based on the Type 114 but used a VW powerplant as promotional fodder for the KdF coupon holders. Porsche

27

The Kübelwagen, *a military version of the people's car, was effective in all kinds of terrain, from the sands of North Africa to the snow and mud of the Russian front. In the later stages of the war even the Allies prized them—the exchange rate in some areas was three Jeeps for one "bucket car."* Porsche

The *"Ferdinand" was a mobile antitank gun, here shown on trials with Albert Speer and Ferdinand Porsche, front right.* Porsche

father were requested by the French to take part in discussions regarding the transfer of the VW designs and factory equipment to France as war reparations and a possible commission to design a French "people's car" with Renault. In December, while meeting with French authorities in Baden-Baden they were arrested, along with Dr. Piëch, and accused of forced-labor practices at the German-run Peugeot plant during the war. The elder Porsche was also accused of instigating the Gestapo arrest of protesting French workers, when actually he had argued for their release. The charges were made by another faction in the French government that did not want a German-designed car to compete with home-grown models.

Ferry Porsche was detained until July 1946, even though the case against him was weak as he had had little connection with the VW plant during the war. But Dr. Porsche and his son-in-law became the pawns in a game of shifting political power in France, and in May 1946 they were moved to Paris where Renault officials took advantage of the "guests" to improve their new 4CV model. By February 1947, any hopes for release were dashed when the men were taken in chains to unheated jail cells in Dijon to suffer through the spring and summer of that year. Until this time, the French had made little effort to get at the truth, but early that year, interviews with people directly involved in wartime operations at Peugeot showed that the men were innocent. They were released on August 1, Dr. Porsche having spent some of his confinement in a prison hospital.

The man who had always displayed such indefatiguable energy would never be the same either in body or spirit. Even after his release, Ferdinand Porsche could still not travel freely, and the charges against him would not be officially dropped for a year. His deteriorating health prevented him from working regularly, but he took an interest in the new projects, providing suggestions and advice when needed. He would live just long enough to see his people's car begin to fill the roads of Germany and the birth of a sports car that carried his own name.

Cisitalia-Porsche Type 360

During the long months that Ferry Porsche was also imprisoned, Louise Piëch had held together the fragmented family organization and was a driving force in the efforts to free her husband and father. Upon Ferry's return, he joined his sister and Karl Rabe in their efforts to free the other men and rebuild the company, but each of these pursuits would require money and repairing surplus Kübelwagens was not the fast track to riches. Design commissions were needed, but who wanted sophisticated automobiles when much of Europe was

28

still buried in rubble? The answer to that question came from Italy.

In the year following the war, the company was eking out an existence in the old sawmill by making water-driven generators and fixing whatever equipment came by the Gmünd shops, providing much-needed employment for more than 200 people. Staff designers were working on new tractors and other agricultural equipment, but with the Austrian economy in ruin, there was no promise that these ideas would ever get beyond the paper stage. The wide network of automotive designers, suppliers and manufacturers around which the racing scene revolved was completely fragmented by the war and in 1946 the house of Porsche was just beginning to reestablish contact with others in the enthusiast field.

Two former Porsche associates, Carlo (Karl) Abarth, a former Austrian dirt-track racer who had fled to Yugoslavia

A rear view of the infamous Cisitalia Formula 1 car. The Type 360 was a racer of untapped potential whose strange career took it from Italy to Germany to Argentina and back. Porsche

before the war, and Rudolf Hruska, a Viennese engineer who had worked for Porsche on the VW and tractor projects during the war, found themselves together in Merano, Italy. They corresponded with Louise Piëch and later, Ferry Porsche, about becoming the firm's agents in Italy. The first work they secured for the Gmünd "factory" came about through a connection with Tazio Nuvolari. Nuvolari was anxious to develop a new Grand Prix car and the two ex-Austrians suggested that Porsche might be able to design such a car. Nuvolari had gone from Alfa Romeo to the Porsche-designed Auto Union in 1938, and he was enthusiastic about the idea.

Abarth and Hruska contacted Ferry Porsche and outlined their plan. The reply came in September 1946: the Porsche organization would design a car for a fee of approximately 100,000 Austrian schillings and oversee its production in Italy. One of the caveats was approval from the various occupation governments for travel, transfer of funds and not the least, inspection of the project to ensure it had no military potential. Porsche had been, after all, one of the German firms at the forefront of military technology, but the Gmünd works were now only interested in battles on the racetrack. The only other obstacle to the project was the matter of financing it, but

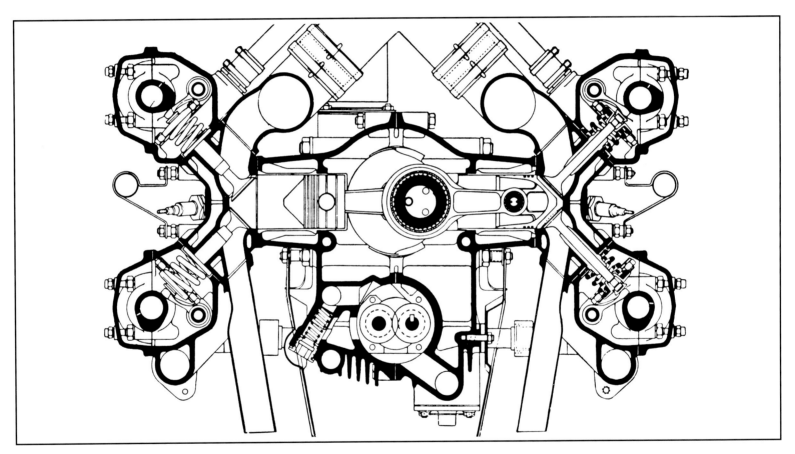

Longitudinal view of the Cisitalia engine shows the radical piston and combustion chamber shape, the counter-balanced Hirth roller-bearing crankshaft and the separate cam housings with finger followers and dual valve springs. Other features included dry-sump lubrication, wet cylinder sleeves without gaskets and dual vane-type blowers. A single spark plug was steeply angled between the two valves and the distributors were driven from the rear of each cam. The bottom line on paper was around 450 hp from 1.5 liters at just more than 10,000 rpm. Aborted development and a lack of adequate

dynamometer equipment in Italy and Argentina left the question of what will this engine really do unanswered. Aside from funding Professor Porsche's freedom, this design, based on the Auto-Union cars of the 1930s, became the pattern for Porsche racing engines for decades to come. The four-cam Type 547 of 1953 and later derivatives used a similar design, adapted to air-cooling. A 1960 drawing of Porsche's Type 753 grand prix eight bears a startling resemblance to the layout shown here. Car and Driver

Nuvolari knew Corrado Millanta, a photographer and journalist well-connected in racing circles. Millanta knew Count Giovanni Lurani, and Lurani suggested that they contact Piero Dusio, an Italian who had recently founded his own car company. Dusio's Cisitalia had already begun production of a small, tube-frame sports racer using Fiat components, but his dream was to compete in Grand Prix racing; he saw this as a golden opportunity. That winter, Abarth and Hruska met with Louise Piëch, Ferry Porsche, Karl Rabe and Hans Kern at an Austrian ski resort and began negotiations that would result in a signed contract on February 2, 1947. The deal was done only after Dusio was assured that the project could be carried out in the absence of Professor Porsche, that he was not designing a similar race car for the French and that the company possessed no similar type of race car design from the Auto Union days that might one day appear on the track to challenge his own.

Dusio hired the Porsche firm to build not only a Grand Prix car, Type 360, but also a sports car, Type 370. The Type 360 Cisitalia, built for the grand prix formula of 1.5 liters, was a racing machine ahead of its time in many ways. A 350 hp flat twelve-cylinder displacing 1498 cc, it featured two shaft-driven overhead camshafts on each cylinder bank with a distributor driven off the rear of each intake cam. Mounted above the engine was a supercharger and two dual-throat Weber carburetors. The roller-bearing crankshaft was built by the Hirth company and connected to a five-speed gearbox with a provision for four-wheel drive, engaged by the driver for grip during acceleration.

The engine was situated amidships, just behind the driver, and saddle fuel tanks at the car's center of gravity assured even balance at any fuel load. The transmission, using a new synchronizing system developed by Leopold Schmid, was between the engine and differential with the torsion bar-sprung rear axle at the very back of the vehicle. The dual lateral torsion bar front suspension was similar to the VW—except for the driveshaft between them. Many ideas in the racer came from the Type 114 Porsche sports car that was never built and many of the same concepts would be carried on with the Type 550 Spyder a few years later.

The Cisitalia Type 370 sports car was an air-cooled six-cylinder, rear-engine four-seater with a pressed-steel pan and five-speed transmission weighing about 1,323 lb. Type 370 never got beyond drawings because Dusio's own sports car became successful in competition and in sales that summer. In addition to these two exotics, Dusio commissioned two other designs that he assumed would find a ready market in the rural areas. One was a small tractor, Type 323, and the other a water turbine for electrical generating, Type 285. Dusio's tractors were never built, but Porsche resumed work on its own designs that had begun with Hitler's *Volkschlepper* ten years earlier. In 1949, the plans were sold to the Allgaier company, which built Porsche-Diesel tractors until 1957.

The new Cisitalia Formula One car was under construction in Turin, Italy, in the summer of 1947 when Ferry Porsche and Karl Rabe visited Dusio's factory. It had taken nine months to secure travel passes but the effort was certainly worthwhile—this trip was to figure importantly in the future of the Porsche company. The visitors saw that the little Cisitalia sports car was made from basic Fiat parts and their conclusion was that Volkswagen parts could be put to the same use. Of course, they had had the same thoughts ten years earlier, but the Nazi government, which "owned" the VW, had stood in their way. Now, it was just a matter of money. Returning to Gmünd, Porsche and Rabe set to work on a new project, a VW-based sports car: light, nimble, affordable and most importantly, inexpensive to build.

Using most of the Cisitalia design fees, Ferry and Louise were able to pay what amounted to ransom: 1 million French francs in order to bail their father and Anton Piëch out of prison. When the Cisitalia plans were shown to the professor, he responded that he wouldn't have done it any differently himself. Prof. Eberan von Eberhorst, who had fled the Russian sector with only the clothes on his back, was hired as a consultant since there were many parallels with the Auto Union project that Eberan von Eberhorst had overseen.

Dusio wanted to begin track testing on the first of a planned six Type 360 cars in the spring of 1948, but the whole undertaking was, by this time, beginning to strain his finances. At the end of that year his company was floating in red ink. By summer 1949, Dusio had liquidated his Italian holdings and was in Argentina where he took up new duties as head of a national auto and truck concern set up by President Juan Peron. Peron had paid off Cisitalia's debts in exchange for a Grand Prix car to wear Argentinian colors, but at this distance from the Gmünd engineers, little development progress was made. It was not until January 1953 that the car was first road tested, for the Buenos Aires Grand Prix, but it was obviously nowhere near ready. That July it was used in an attempt to break a local speed record during which a piston was holed and the car ended up, almost forgotten, in a small garage. It was saved from an ignominious fate in 1959 when Porsche returned it to Stuttgart to become a centerpiece in the *werks* museum that opened that year. So the ultimate racing car never turned a wheel in competition, but the men who created it had little time to reflect on its fate—they were busy with another new car that *would* leave its mark in racing annals for decades yet to come.

Chapter 3

Beginnings in Gmünd

Genesis in a Sawmill

The long-considered idea of a VW-based sports car came to fruition under the designation Type 356. The first Porsche model to bear its designer's name was completed in early June 1948. Chassis drawings date from July 1947, and show a space frame welded from steel tubing, à la Cisitalia. The open roadster body went through a design period of almost a year, and some of the first drawings bring to mind a carnival bumper car. But the fifth and final design was clean

Porsche, Gmünd, 1948
Seen outside Porsche's Gmünd "factory," the first Type 356/2 Gmünd coupe and the original Type 356 roadster. Both cars used the two-piece flat-glass windshields, although the roadster's did not have a frame around the glass. The cars' license plate numbers—K49 801 for the coupe and K45 286 for the roadster—have gone down in history. Porsche

and virtually free of ornamentation. Bumpers were fitted flush with the body, and worn proudly across its nose was the name Porsche in extended block letters which, in similar form, are still used today. Erwin Komenda was responsible for the car's shape, which made use of lessons learned with the prewar Berlin-Rome racers. He was gifted with an instinctive feel for aerodynamic efficiency, which is seen in this and later models of the 356 line. Total dry weight was just more than 1,300 lb. The interior furnishings included a speedometer, a clock built into the glovebox and a flat bench seat with a rather upright backrest. The doorsills were high and wide, giving a pronounced low-slung feel. The engine lid opened as a unit, and had narrow slots along its outer edges; a stylish, yet marginal solution to the engine's need for cooling air.

Mechanically, the car was almost pure Volkswagen: steering, 9 in. cable-operated drum brakes, front suspension and a non-synchronized four-speed transmission. The most obvious departure from its VW origin was the placement of the engine in front of the transaxle. This arrangement had its precedent in Porsche's Auto Union Grand Prix cars of the 1930s, and the engineers felt it allowed the best weight distribution for handling. Using the VW rear suspension, however, was a bit ticklish. The transverse torsion bar tube and trailing arms that in the production VW were ahead of the engine, were turned around and placed at the rear of the engine-transmission assembly resulting in leading arms in the Porsche. Consequently, the rear tires had a tendency to toe out under suspension movement or cornering, increasing oversteer. It was an unwelcome state of affairs, but was mitigated somewhat by the lightness of the car. One of the first passengers to ride in the finished chassis, Eberan von Eberhorst, was impressed and he urged Ferry Porsche to move ahead with the project.

Porsche 356-001

The people at Porsche had supreme confidence in the VW components used in the new car. After all, Kübelwagens had put on millions of miles under extreme circumstances during

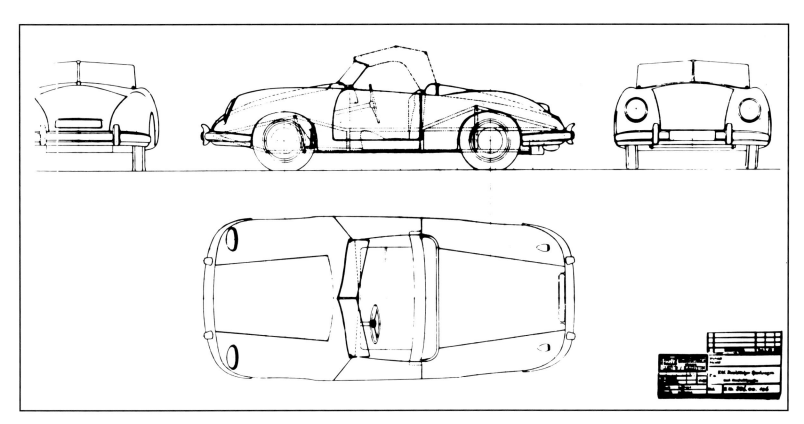

One of the blueprint drawings for the first Porsche Type 356 roadster. The contours were simple to facilitate the panel-beating process. Porsche

the war. The engine used in civilian VWs after the war displaced 1131 cc and produced 25 hp with a 5.8:1 compression ratio. The Porsche engineers already had a dozen years of experience hot-rodding the people's powerplant, and the improvements they made for the new sports car were relatively modest: intake and exhaust valves were slightly enlarged and the compression ratio was increased to 7.0:1. This last change was rather optimistic, since the locally available fuels were extremely low grade.

The engine was installed in the chassis and it was tested, sans body, in March of 1948. The body was then hand-built over a period of two months by a former Austro-Daimler coachbuilder, Friedrich Weber. He was an exquisite craftsman, but fond of drink, and stories of production coming to a standstill while he recovered from a weekend bout serve to illustrate just one of the many obstacles that the company faced in Gmünd.

While on an early test drive up the Grossglockner Pass, one of the car's rear suspension members bent from the rough pavement. Ferry Porsche and his passenger, an engineer named Rupilius, found some angle iron at a nearby road maintenance shop and in a few hours had effected a repair and were back on their way. The mountain breakdown was the only failure that occurred in testing, and that makeshift fix is still a part of 356–001 today.

David Scott-Moncrieff, an English engineer and author, was one of the first foreign visitors to reach the remote village after the first car was built. In an article written for *Porsche Panorama*, the magazine of the Porsche Club of America, he described his impressions of driving 356–001: "I was absolutely shattered by its roadholding. . . . to find this new prototype as taut and road-hugging as a Grand Prix Bugatti was an incredible experience. . . . I cannot say very much about the performance, because every time I put my foot down, the poor

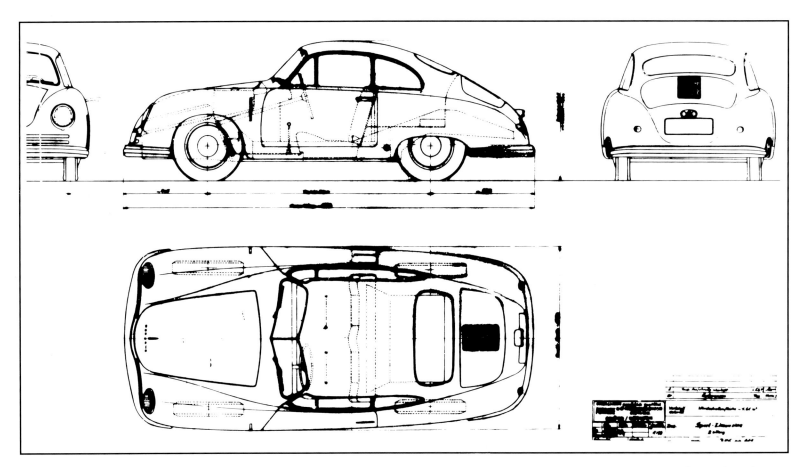

Erwin Komenda's body design for the 356/2 followed the architect's creed, "form follows function." Light weight and smooth contours would contribute to the car's reputation for speedy, yet frugal transport. Porsche

little flat four engine knocked like an anvil chorus. This was due to the fact that the only gas they could get was Russian, which, at that time, was very near kerosene." It is likely Moncrieff did not push the car hard, but his comments illustrated the favorable reviews that would be given by other journalists in the coming months.

The car was never intended for series production, but it served well in the role of selling a concept. A Swiss advertising agency owner, R. von Senger, had previously contracted with the firm to design an automobile, Porsche Type 352. He knew of the sports car plans, and saw the first roadster under construction at Gmünd. He showed his enthusiasm by ordering five cars.

Von Senger's involvement with Porsche would be crucial for many reasons. He and an associate, Swiss automobile dealer Bernhard Blank, provided not only firm orders for *Porsche Konstruktionen's* vehicles, but were the source of much of the material needed to build the cars. Austrians faced severe restrictions in import and export, currency and travel activities, but the Swiss "partners" could supply VW parts, aluminum and other materials from far and wide. The government in Vienna granted to Porsche import licenses for certain materials, but only with the understanding that all cars manufactured would be sold abroad, to bring in foreign currency. With von Senger's backing, production plans for the new model went ahead as quickly as possible, albeit on a limited scale.

A light, nimble two-seater was by no means a unique idea, and Porsche was not the only company to use the VW as a basis for a sporting machine. In Vienna, Wolfgang Denzel was

Porsche, Gmünd, 1948
The first coupe and progenitor of the Porsche line, 356/2 was built on a steel chassis that was ready for the road in July 1948. A smiling

Ferry Porsche, center, could never have foreseen more than 76,000 of these cars being built in the next sixteen years. Porsche

35

building a vehicle that, at first glance, could easily be mistaken for the mid-engine Porsche, and Petermax Müller, in Potsdam, Germany, was racing aluminum-bodied cars using VW engines with war-surplus attack-boat high-performance cylinder heads. But the Gmünd company had the advantage of a respected name and this first car showed that they could do it right. Within a month of completion, von Senger arranged for the car to be shown and demonstrated to a number of journalists before the Swiss Grand Prix in Bern, and their reports quickly found their way into the motoring press across the Continent. The little roadster was also pressed into racing service that July, and won its class at a local race in Innsbruck with Herbert Kaes at the wheel. As important as this seminal vehicle was, however, one could say it was obsolete before it was completed, and in fact, the sale of the car had been arranged before it first rolled out of the Gmünd shops.

Porsche 356-002

Ferry Porsche had learned many lessons from the 356-001 prototype. It was apparent that the space-frame concept would not allow the kind of construction efficiency necessary for volume production, and a mid-engine layout left precious little cargo room. And so, even as the first roadster was being built, work began on 356-002, a coupe. This next car would share the type number but not much else.

Forming the basis of the 356-002 was a welded steel chassis that roughly corresponded to the VW floor pan, but was much stronger. Box-section sills and a center tunnel stiffened the flat floor longitudinally, and angled panels joined the front bulkhead area with a larger flat box that angled down slightly, forming the nose of the chassis. Enclosed in this forward structure were the footwells, suspension and steering components. As in the VW, fitting just in front of the dash area was the fuel tank. At the rear, a smaller flat shelf above the axle became the rear seat and luggage area, bracing the vertical arched panels that formed the inner wheelwells. This entire chassis assembly could be lifted by two men with ease.

The torsion bar tube was welded in place near the rear of the floor pan and formed the basis for the transmission mounts. The engine was back in the VW position, behind the transaxle, and the added weight offset would give new meaning to the term oversteer for a generation of Porsche drivers. But at least with this layout the rear suspension trailing arms could work the way they were designed. VW cable-operated drum brakes were installed, but on the later Gmünd cars, Lockheed of England supplied the twin-leading-shoe hydraulic front drum brakes. Single-acting tube shocks were used in front and lever arm shocks at the rear, with 5x16 in. tires.

The rolling chassis was ready for testing in July 1948, and was thoroughly pummeled over local roads before being fitted with a body that is immediately recognizable even today as a Porsche. The body panels were formed by hand from aluminum sheets on a wooden buck, with the doors being fashioned from steel. The V-shaped two-piece windshield was complemented by side vent windows that pivoted open, though the rear quarter windows were fixed. Later Gmünd coupes would feature curved, fixed vent windows on the doors; the operable vents would return some years later. Inside, the two matching dash panels housed on the left a speedometer and switches, and on the right a glovebox with clock. The bench seat and fixed seatback were rather Spartan, and the gearshift rod and torsion bar tube were visible in the cabin. These last two items would soon be incorporated under sheet metal. At the rear, the engine lid carried rather fussy slots with three trim pieces, and the license plate area was flattened more than on the later cars. As on its roadster cousin, the bumpers were smoothly integrated below the bodywork. The nose trim consisted of a horizontal strip connecting two small turn signals, but these and the rear turn signal lights would be replaced by swing-out turn indicators on some subsequent cars.

Concurrently under development was a new version of the VW engine, dubbed the Type 369. The basic power unit as used in the Volkswagen was, at 25 hp, understressed to ensure long life and the main constraint on increased performance was its breathing ability. In order to enlarge the valves, the Porsche engineers canted the exhaust valves outward at 32 deg. on the horizontal plane. This also smoothed the flow from the sharp angle in the VW exhaust port and afforded better cooling of the head. Dual valve springs allowed higher revs, and each head received its own 26 mm Solex carburetor. Domed pistons gave a published 7.0:1 compression ratio in the 1131 cc engine, producing 40 hp at 4000 rpm. A slightly smaller bore of 73.5 mm was used in some engines to bring them under the popular 1100 race classification at 1086 cc. With slightly less compression, the same horsepower was reached at 4200 rpm. Though the engines didn't have impressive power figures, the aerodynamic vehicles could reach 88 mph and return more than 30 mpg in the bargain.

Gmünd Coupes and Beutler Cabriolets

In the summer of 1948, the first promotional material was published in Vienna. A drawing showed the limousine (coupe) and cabriolet versions with specifications in German, English and French. Bernhard Blank was also readying a specification sheet to accompany the prototype coupe on display in his showroom. Blank's *Kreuzgarage* in Zurich then displayed a bare chassis, and two more chassis were delivered to the

Beutler brothers' workshop outside of Bern. Von Senger had arranged to have convertible bodies built on the frames, and one was finished in time for the March 1949 Swiss Auto Show in Geneva. It shared a corner of the hall with a Gmünd coupe, the first international showing of the cars.

The Beutler cabriolets were well finished and, with slight exceptions, followed the lines of the aluminum coupe. The rear portion was more square with a large relief area for license, and slight fender bulges were evident behind the doors. The interior featured nicely paneled doors and a large speedometer

Some of the first cabriolets were built in Switzerland by Karosserie Beutler, using chassis shipped from Gmünd. The Beutler bodies were *distinguished by a slightly bulged rear fender, and were quite well finished. Porsche*

and clock on the left and right, respectively, with switches in the center of the dash. Beutler would make four more cabriolets in 1949, and Porsche also produced two cabriolets that year. Total 1949 production in Gmünd was recorded as twenty-five cars, with another eighteen being built in 1950. Four cars were built in 1951, with the last going to Otto Mathé of Innsbruck.

The cars were not cheap—the price was the equivalent of some $4,000—but into the fold came many wealthy enthusiasts who lent credence to Porsche's claims of quality design and construction. Among the earliest customers were many whose names were preceded by titles and letters including an Egyptian, Prince Abd el Monheim. Although one can assume he was not a typical Porsche customer, he thoroughly enjoyed his car, the thirty-fifth. Richard von Frankenberg, the unofficial Porsche historian, wrote, "The Prince was fairly fat and, so as not to rub against the lower edge of the steering wheel, he always spread a large silk handkerchief . . . between his shirt and the steering wheel and as a matter of fact he was quite a good driver." Word spread quickly about the new sports car, and the sawmill factory found that demand was beginning to exceed their ability to produce. Many of the first cars were delivered in Switzerland and Austria, but Scania-Vabis in Sweden took most of the 1950 production. In autumn 1948, Chief Engineer Karl Rabe told a Vienna newspaper that the factory would deliver 150 units to Switzerland by the year's end. He overestimated by 146, and in fact, only fifty cars

would leave Gmünd over a period of three years. But even the optimistic Dr. Rabe couldn't foresee the thousands of cars that were to come.

The public's acceptance of the new model was a mixed blessing for Porsche. The workers at Gmünd had to contend with primitive conditions: many of the company's machine tools had disappeared after the war, the nearest rail line was twelve miles distant and every part was difficult to obtain. The phrase hand-built was used with pride in Porsche's advertising, but one can assume they would have welcomed just a little more mechanization.

A Firm Footing for the New Company

In 1948, the winds of change were swirling around the village of Gmünd and beyond, all across Europe. At about the same time the first Porsche saw the light of day, the new German Deutschmark came into being. Trade restrictions were eased, and with the introduction of the Marshall Plan, the economy of the entire region began a slow renewal. The Porsche organization was also on the uphill road to recovery. They spent the immediate postwar period repairing what machinery came to the door of the Gmünd shops, and in three years had progressed to the design of tractors, water turbine generators and other projects that were beginning to show a profit. Since the manufacture of sports cars in such small quantities was not particularly lucrative, Ferry Porsche was in contact with the Austrian government and certain large financial concerns to try to obtain the financial backing that could allow expansion. While the Austrian government was anxious for Porsche to succeed, none of the established car makers in that country were. By the spring of 1949, Ferry Porsche decided that an arrangement with the Volkswagen organization would best suit Porsche's needs.

The Volkswagen plant at Wolfsburg was little more than a smoking ruin at war's end, but the British, in whose zone the factory lay, were quick to resume production. A number of American and British car makers were offered the plant and its products, in essence, for free. They all refused; who needed the headaches of a bombed-out plant and a strange little car? But the British army kept production bumping along, building cars for its troops' use, until Heinz Nordhoff was given the job of general manager in 1948. Nordhoff, former head of Opel trucks, had little regard for, or knowledge of, the VW. However, he was an able administrator and a man of vision, and he had met the younger Porsche during the war. So when Ferry contacted him in the spring of 1949, the two were able to lay the groundwork for an agreement that would be of great benefit to both sides. On September 16, Ferry Porsche met with Nordhoff and negotiated a contract that was signed the

From left, Karl Rabe, Erwin Komenda and Ferry Porsche, the key players in the company's growth and creators of a legendary car. Porsche

next day. The many-faceted agreement included engineering services, parts and auto sales, and it was a landmark for the Stuttgart company.

The Porsche organization was retained, once again, as consultants for design work, bringing a much-needed infusion of cash but effectively preventing them from doing any work on a competitor's car. Porsche would also receive a small royalty payment for each VW produced and in exchange would be able to easily acquire the parts needed to build their sports cars. Once the cars were built, they could be sold and serviced through the VW network of dealers. Each of these points would benefit both parties for the next two decades. A further development took place in May 1949 when *Porsche Salzburg* was established as the sole agent for the sale and service of Volkswagens in Austria. Ferry's sister Louise, her husband Anton Piëch and cousin Herbert Kaes were the principals. The venture started out slowly, with only fourteen VWs imported to Austria that year, but the foundation was laid. For the first time since the war, it appeared that the house of Porsche was once again on solid ground.

Porsche, Gmünd, 1948
The Gmünd cars were completely hand built. The finished product belied the fact that it was constructed in a crude shed with limited equipment. Porsche

39

Porsche, Zuffenhausen, 1951

At the time this photo was taken, Porsche employed eight engine assemblers, each of whom had complete responsibility for the finished powerplant that came from their bench. Working at the rate of about one engine a day, they meticulously checked all tolerances, stamped their initials on the case and sent their engines off to be run on a dynamometer for two hours or more. Technicians in nearby areas did preparatory work such as polishing head ports, lapping valves, weighing and matching rods, boring the cases and balancing the crankshaft-flywheel assembly on a high speed jig. Visitors commented that this part of the Porsche factory resembled a race shop more than an auto assembly line. Tom Countryman

Chapter 4

Zuffenhausen Redux

Porsche's Return to Germany

The automobile manufacturing part of the company, Porsche Konstruktionen, had an uncertain future at the end of 1949. While the cars themselves were gaining wide acceptance, there was no guarantee that it would ever be a money-making operation. It was obvious that the difficulties in Gmünd would never allow any real quantity or profit margin, so the only logical way to make the enterprise work was to move back to Stuttgart. Some members of the Porsche and Piëch families thought that a return to design and development pursuits was the best course for the company; manufacturing cars required enormous commitments, and there were other, possibly more lucrative things to build. An additional complication arose in the form of German taxes: Porsche was accumulating income from the VW payments and the rent on its Zuffenhausen works, which the American army had taken over and maintained as a motor pool. Porsche's business manager Albert Prinzing advised that the company begin production of something, *anything*, in Germany to offset this income.

There was no money to buy another building in Stuttgart. Porsche already owned a complex that was well suited to its purposes, but no one could tell when the Americans would vacate. The army's cavalier attitude was well known to Prof. Porsche; when he had visited Zuffenhausen in 1947, the old man had asked to look around his building, but General Funk, the American commander, refused to even see him. It was not until the fall of 1949 that Ferry Porsche heard any encouraging news concerning the buildings. The mayor of Stuttgart, Dr. Klett, was told that the army may vacate by as early as the next July. Anxious to begin the move, the company sent an administrative contingent to Stuttgart where initial plans were begun for the transfer of automobile design and assembly work. This group included Prinzing, Karl Kirn, who had been looking after Porsche's interests in Stuttgart, and thirty-six-year old Hans Klauser, who would become head of produc-

tion. They took up their new tasks in the place that had given birth to the Volkswagen—the garage and cook's quarters of the Porsche family villa on the Fuerbacher Weg.

Back on the "assembly line" in Gmünd, completed chassis often had to wait while the bodies were completed. To avoid such bottlenecks, it was decided that before production resumed in Germany, a supplier for bodies would be chosen from among the many karosserien in the area. Dr. Porsche was influential; he pointed out that aside from a monetary concern, Reutter had the best craftsmen. These craftsmen did not, however, have the necessary skills and equipment to weld aluminum, so a change to steel bodies was

Porsche, Zuffenhausen, 1950
Hans Klauser (center, with tie) joins a group of proud workmen beside the first Porsche completed in Stuttgart, in March 1950. This 356 was a light grey coupe named the Windhund. Porsche

The layout was standardized for production of the new steel-bodied German cars. Although the car would be continuously improved in *the next fourteen years, the basic design followed this 1951 drawing.* Porsche

made. The Porsche management team estimated, from previous orders and the reaction at auto shows, that 500 units could be sold at a production rate of nine cars a month. In November 1949, Reutter was given an order for 500 bodies.

Reutter, a long-established Stuttgart firm, had built prototypes for the Porsche Design Bureau in the 1930s and was able

to remain in business after the devastation of war by doing bodywork on private cars in their Zuffenhausen shop and by repairing streetcars in their buildings on the west side of the city. It was here that the first prototype bare-metal body was made and rolled-out into the daylight of a late winter day in 1950. Both Porsches inspected the vehicle and after a few minutes the elder man asked for a chair. He sat looking at the front of the car long enough to start everyone wondering if he

An Interview with Ferdinand Porsche

This is an excerpt from an interview granted by Ferdinand Porsche, general manager of the Porsche factory in Stuttgart, Germany, to Samuel Weill, associate editor of *Road & Track* on December 19, 1950.

What is the present production rate of the Porsche factory?
Six cars a day.
What are the production plans of the Porsche factory for the future?
The Porsche car is a handmade special car. The Porsche firm is first and foremost a design and consulting engineering firm. For this reason, they are not particularly interested in raising their production, since they want to keep on making fine handmade cars.
Why is the design of the present Porsche car as it is? How is the high cost of the car justified?
The design of the car evolved from the experience acquired

with the Auto-Union car. The air-cooling system was installed because of the good experience with the VW car. Porsche wanted to build a car in which the experience gained from the Auto-Union and VW cars would be combined. The price of the car is justified in Germany because of the high quality and excellent design of the car. One cannot mass produce a high-quality handmade car. If the car were to be mass produced, it would not be as good. The Porsche factory makes six handmade cars a day, which is a pretty good production rate in Europe. The car's body is comparable to the Pinin Farina bodies, and is much cheaper for what it is than any made anywhere else.
Are cars of all the German makes available to all German citizens?
In Germany anyone can buy any German car. Of course, the delivery varies. For example, one has to wait six months to take delivery of a VW. Other makes, whose name I do not wish to mention, can make delivery of their models immediately.

had fallen asleep. Suddenly, he came out of his reverie exclaiming that the car was not symmetrical! A measurement of the body showed that the old professor still had a keen eye—it was just over half an inch wider on the right. After this problem was resolved, the body was sent for final assembly to the Reutter Zuffenhausen shop where Porsche had rented a little more than 5,000 sq-ft as a final assembly area. The finished product, a light grey coupe dubbed *Windhund*, rolled out on April 6 and went into service as Ferry Porsche's personal car. Production was officially under way.

The car manufacturing business was a costly enterprise, however, and the VW license fees could not cover all the new subcontracting expenses. Albert Prinzing took to the road in a Gmünd demonstrator, accompanied by a Beutler cabriolet, and made the rounds of VW dealers who were meeting at Wolfsburg. His sales pitch was unique and effective: each dealer would pay in advance for the *last* car delivered to them. Prinzing returned to Stuttgart with thirty-seven firm orders and $50,000 to launch the new start in Porsche's old home.

With the company located once again in Germany, the job of making meaningful long-range plans began. Soon after assembly operations started in a corner of the Reutter building, a small brick shed nearby was also put to use as an engine assembly area. It was an improvement over the sawmill in

Paris Auto Show, 1950
At the Paris show in 1950, Porsche celebrated fifty years of automobile design. It was here that Max Hoffman met with the Professor and cemented a relationship that would last for years. The seed was also planted here that would grow into many victories at Le Mans. Porsche

Karosserie Reutter, Zuffenhausen, 1951
A chassis takes shape. An old story maintains that the craftsmen building Porsches were paid by the number of welds. True or not, there was no skimping on the strength of joints in the body. Courtesy George Wilke

Austria, but the workers from Gmünd found that the nickname, "Amalgamated Hut Works," still applied. When the American army was put on full alert in June with the outbreak of war in Korea, Porsche became less hopeful of the imminent return of their original buildings, and purchased an 1,100 sq-ft wooden barracks nearby. In this building the engineering and administration staff took up their work in December 1950.

Along with this change of address came a new company name and organizational structure. Dr. -Ing. h.c. F. Porsche KG, a limited partnership, replaced the former Porsche Konstruktionen GmbH. This new entity followed more closely the structure of Porsche's original Design Bureau as laid out twenty years before.

While still in Gmünd, Erwin Komenda had been at work on drawings that smoothed the contours of the new steel body. Subtle changes were made in the sweep of the fender line from front to rear, the hood line and shape were new and the Porsche script was now below the hood opening. The two-piece windshield was extended and curved at its sides. The curved side vent windows were dropped (opening vents would appear again in 1958) and the rear quarter windows were fixed in their rubber moldings. Features inside included

Karosserie Reutter, Zuffenhausen, 1951
The shaped body panels were attached to the chassis in a body jig. Courtesy George Wilke

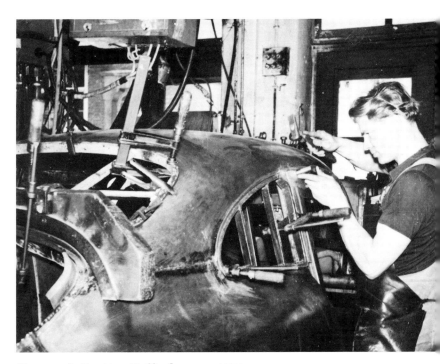

Karosserie Reutter, Zuffenhausen, 1951
Metal finishing was carried out by hand on seams and edges. Courtesy George Wilke

44

large bucket seats, beech door trim and basic instrumentation: speedometer and clock or optional tachometer. Polished trim pieces with rubber inserts ran along the bumpers, which sometimes sported upright horns for protection.

Carrying over from the last Gmünd cars, the new Type 369, 1.1 liter engine was used, with dual Solex 32 PBI single-barrel carbs. Each engine was built by a single journeyman who stamped his initials on the crankcase; after some twenty-five hours building one engine, a man had a right to sign his "work of art." But pride and responsibility were two sides of the same coin, as an assembler would soon learn if a sick engine came back for repair. These powerplants operated at a 7.0:1 compression ratio and Porsche urged owners to mix Benzol with their gas to increase the octane rating. Some 40 hp could now be achieved with reliability, although certain other parts of the car, like the brakes, demanded care.

Gmünd cars had used front twin-leading-shoe drum brakes supplied by the English Lockheed company, but Alfred Teves was the German licensee for these and could not supply them to Porsche. VW had in the meantime adopted new hydraulic brakes which were also fitted to the first Zuffen-hausen Porsches, but stopping power was still a weak link in the chain.

The other item most commonly faulted was the VW-based transmission. With its unsynchronized gears, it needed a break-in period before it could be used quietly, and even then required a sensitive hand. Factory mechanics talked about testing the shifting skills of each prospective buyer to see if they "deserved" a Porsche. This proprietary attitude was half joking, but reflected both the pride that workers felt and the fact that the cars simply weren't meant for everyone.

Sunset for the Old Master

September 3, 1950, marked the seventy-fifth birthday of Ferdinand Porsche. A celebration was held at Schloss Soli-tude near Stuttgart—the estate is familiar to anyone who has seen Porsche advertising brochures over the years as many new models were photographed there. Lined up near the stately castle steps were Porsche cars from all over Germany. Their owners, along with such notables as Rudolf Caracciola, had come to honor the man who did so much to advance the state of the art in motoring. A birthday gift, a new 356 coupe, was presented to the professor. Later named *Ferdinand* and

Karosserie Reutter, Zuffenhausen, 1951
Careful sanding and leading filled the seams where body parts joined. Door, trunk and engine lid seams were filled and filed to maintain a consistent 3 mm clearance. Courtesy George Wilke

Karosserie Reutter, Zuffenhausen, 1951
Wet sanding of the metal and paint assured a smooth finish. Courtesy George Wilke

used for years as a test vehicle, the car can be seen today in the Porsche museum.

In October, the senior Porsche traveled to Paris with his nephew Ghislaine Kaes in the *Windhund* to attend the Salon de l'Automobile. The two Porsche cars on display were under a simple banner that commemorated a half-century since the first Porsche-designed automobile. It was in 1900 that the Lohner-Porsche had been shown in Paris, the beginning of a long tradition.

At the 1950 show, a French race driver and exotic car dealer, Auguste Veuillet, was looking at the Porsches on display with particular interest. He was enthusiastic about the cars and, like a number of others, was eager to secure the distribution rights in his country. He also suggested entering Le Mans, and later that month, the Porsches were visited by Charles Faroux, a well-known figure in the French racing world, who invited them to take part in the next twenty-four-hour event.

This prospect of international acclaim in racing was important to the old man, but probably no more so than the universal acceptance of his people's car. In November, he went to visit the Wolfsburg factory where he witnessed the amazing rebirth of both a factory and a dream. For here was the fulfillment of an idea he had nurtured for decades—a true people's automobile. Ferdinand Porsche lived to see it, but just barely. The day after he returned to Stuttgart, he suffered a stroke that left him partially paralyzed. Nursed at home, and later at a Stuttgart hospital, he made little improvement. He died on January 30, 1951, and was laid to rest at the family estate at Zell-am-See. His family and friends would miss him, but there was no danger of this man's place in the history of the automobile being lost. The car and the company that were his legacy were now poised on the brink of success.

Karosserie Reutter, Zuffenhausen, 1951
Thick undercoating helped protect the metal and insulate against road and engine noise. In later lightweight versions, undercoating was deleted. Courtesy George Wilke

Karosserie Reutter, Zuffenhausen, 1951
Outside the Reutter building, three coupes wait to be moved to the rented Porsche space where mechanical components were installed. The impeccable finish prompted Max Hoffman to describe the car as the "German automotive jewel." Courtesy George Wilke

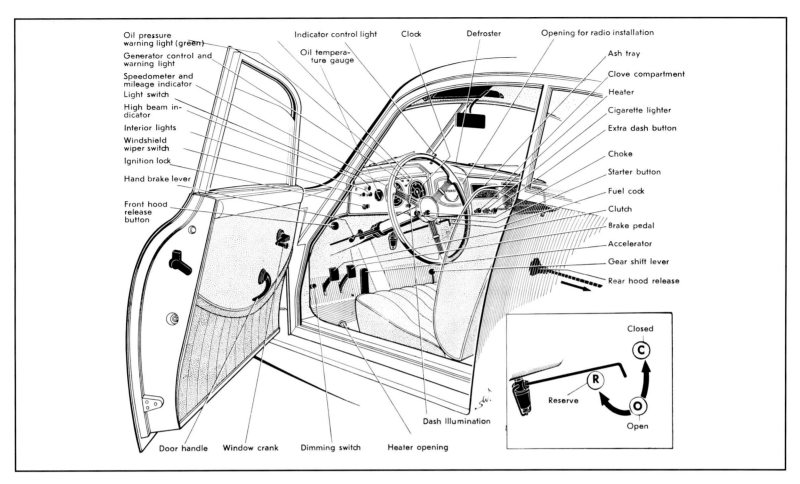

Oil pressure warning light (green)
Generator control and warning light
Speedometer and mileage indicator
Light switch
High beam indicator
Interior lights
Windshield wiper switch
Ignition lock
Hand brake lever
Front hood release button

Indicator control light
Oil temperature gauge
Clock
Defroster
Opening for radio installation

Ash tray
Clove compartment
Heater
Cigarette lighter
Extra dash button
Choke
Starter button
Fuel cock
Clutch
Brake pedal
Accelerator
Gear shift lever
Rear hood release

Door handle
Window crank
Dimming switch
Heater opening
Dash Illumination

Closed
C
R
Reserve
O
Open

In the 1951 Porsches, the tachometer was conspicuous in its absence. It replaced the clock in the 1953 models, along with numerous other dashboard changes. Porsche

The spare tire took up what space was available in the trunk, a condition that was only somewhat improved with the 1953 models. Porsche

Next page
Engine access was never a strong point of the 356 series. Engine lids changed size and shape with different models over the years, but never got much larger and mechanics developed a braille method for many procedures. Like the VW, valves are adjusted from under the car. The later Carrera engine exacerbated the problem; service personnel joked about needing an asbestos octopus to change the plugs. Porsche

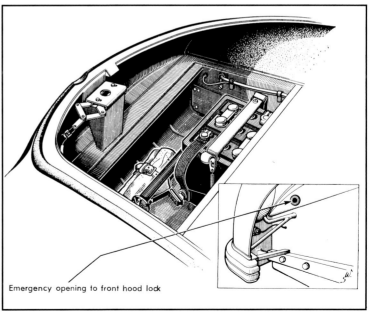

Emergency opening to front hood lock

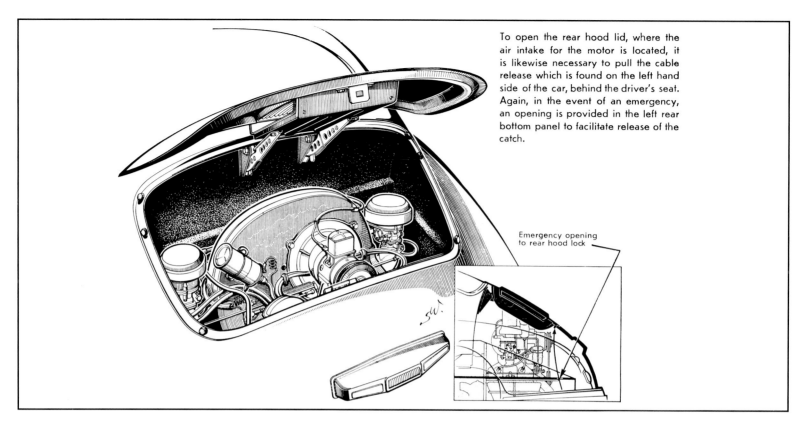

To open the rear hood lid, where the air intake for the motor is located, it is likewise necessary to pull the cable release which is found on the left hand side of the car, behind the driver's seat. Again, in the event of an emergency, an opening is provided in the left rear bottom panel to facilitate release of the catch.

Emergency opening to rear hood lock

The 356 chassis could stand alone, but its rigidity was increased substantially with the body welded on. Although continual changes were made during the 356 series lifetime, the basic design was not changed from this 1951 drawing. These beautifully detailed, yet concise illustrations by Siegfried Werner were typical of the care taken in manuals, advertising and the company magazine, Christophorus, edited by Richard von Frankenberg. Porsche

Chapter 5

Porsche in the United States

The World Market Beckons

Maximillian Edwin Hoffman was a Viennese emigré and auto enthusiast who came to the United States in 1941 with a novel idea for the time: to sell European cars to Americans. His initial plans were sidetracked by the war, but he made ends meet by manufacturing plated-plastic jewelry, an enterprise he started with a borrowed $300 and limited English. By war's end he had accumulated enough capital to go shopping for automotive inventory in Europe, but he found the car makers in both England and on the Continent barely functioning. When in 1947 he finally opened a sales office on Park Avenue in New York, there was but a single Delahaye on the display floor.

Hoffman was determined, and soon many other makes were available from Hoffman Motor Cars—Healey, Citröen and the new Jaguar XK120 among others. With the latter, Americans soon developed a love-hate affair; Hoffman could hardly keep up with Jaguar demand, but breakdowns were so commonplace that he had to get an unlisted phone at home after irate customers began to call him in the small hours of the morning.

As the car makers on the Continent began to rebuild their factories and their business, German and Italian makes also appeared in his showrooms. In July 1950, Hoffman took delivery of twenty Volkswagens and for three years put his considerable talents into promoting it. But the "beetle" was just too different, too small and brought to mind the opposing side in an all-too-recent war. Uncharacteristically, Hoffman gave up on the VW just before its sales began to take off.

By 1950, Hoffman had seen photos of another German product, the new Porsche automobile. He knew the old professor's reputation well and in subsequent correspondence with the Porsche firm in Gmünd and Stuttgart, arrangements were made for three cars to be sent to the United States. They arrived, along with a number of spare parts, in the early fall of

Hoffman, New York, 1950s
A new Max Hoffman showroom on Park Avenue was designed in 1954 by Frank Lloyd Wright to showcase Jaguars. A spiraling ramp led to a raised observation area where cars could be seen from above. Originally, the revolving turntable was to be mirrored so customers could see under the cars, and in the round raised center would be a large gilded Jaguar. But Hoffman had taken on the Mercedes line and in doing so, alienated William Lyons of Jaguar. By the time the showroom was finished, the Jaguar statue and the Jaguar cars were gone. Porsche shared space with BMW, Alfa Romeo and later, Mercedes-Benz. Porsche

that year. Hoffman was pleased when the small cars generated a lot of interest at a pre-race concours at Watkins Glen, New York, and serious racers like Briggs Cunningham, who bought one of these first imports, were enthusiastic.

The next step was to meet with Porsche, but even five years after the war had ended, travel by Germans was restricted, so Hoffman went to the Paris Auto show in October 1950 and met Dr. Porsche and Albert Prinzing. Though he had serious reservations about the car's shape and its appeal to American buyers, Hoffman responded to Ferry Porsche's estimation of perhaps five cars a year in the United States by stating, "If I can't sell five cars a week, I'm not interested!" An agency agreement was reached and he not only began to sell the cars, but raced, promoted and almost single-handedly built the early reputation of Porsche in the United States. Hoffman Motor Cars imported thirty-two cars in 1951 and in just a few more years was selling 30 percent of Zuffenhausen's output. Karl Ludvigsen, in an article about Hoffman, stated,

Hoffman, New York, 1950s
The Broadway showroom of Hoffman, Inc., was the launching point for the XK 120 Jaguar, a sleek roadster billed as the "fastest stock car in the world." The other side of the Jaguar equation was a pathetic record of breakdowns and repairs that kept Hoffman's mechanics busy and his phone ringing off the hook with complaints. He had a considerably easier time servicing the pushrod Porsches. Early on, he sold whatever was available from European car builders, which in 1950 was mostly English makes. The same year this photo was taken he introduced the country to the Volkswagen, but Americans were not interested—at least not yet. Porsche

"From the beginning of Porsche car manufacturing the role of Hoffman and the American market was central to the make's success."

The road to success in the United States was paved with obstacles, however, not the least of which was the price. A small, four-cylinder, air-cooled, rear-engine car with a strange shape was not an easy sell to people who were used to Fords and Plymouths—and for the $4,000 it took to buy the car from Stuttgart, you could have both of those sedans. But servicemen returning from Europe were bringing back cars that were unlike any Chevy they had driven at home. MGs and Jaguars from England paved the way, and 1950 was just the beginning of a wave of foreign cars that would swell over the United States in years to come. "Maxie," as Hoffman was known in the trade, recognized that the Porsche automobile, with its "jewel-like finish" had a feel of quality that could justify the price to those who appreciated a well-designed and well-executed piece of machinery. Although the early cars seem crude and fragile by today's standards, they consistently outperformed larger, more powerful machines on the racetracks, often with Max Hoffman himself at the wheel.

The bulk of his business was selling Jaguars at the time and the new XK120 was a sleek beauty, but the heavy handling and spotty build quality were a disappointment to Hoffman, though that didn't keep customers from standing in line to order them. He tried to arrange for the British company's chairman William Lyons to let Porsche consult on the engineering of a new Jaguar, but neither Lyons nor Porsche was enthusiastic and nothing came of it. Hoffman would do the same thing a year later when he made a suggestion to his friend Richard Hutchinson, a vice president of Studebaker. Hoffman could see that in the US car market, the postwar feeding frenzy would soon end and tiny Studebaker would be unable to compete with the Big Three. He sensed the almost unlimited demand for a small, efficient VW-type car. His idea was to have Studebaker market something the Big Three didn't have—an "American Volkswagen"—and who better to design such a vehicle than Porsche?

The American Connection

Ferry Porsche came to the United States in December 1951, his first trip across the ocean since 1937. It was his first airplane flight, necessitated by a short-notice appointment with the Mid-American Research Corporation, which was interested in developing a small Jeep-like vehicle for airborne troops. The meetings with the American company bore no fruit for the Porsche company, but Ferry was able to visit Hoffman's Park Avenue showroom, where he was suitably impressed by Hoffman's style and marketing savvy.

The next spring, Porsche was contacted by Wendell Fletcher, whose California-based aviation company had plans to produce a similar Jeep for the US Army. This vehicle would use a number of Porsche components and would be a large enough project to justify another trip to the United States. Another American company, Gyrodyne of Long Island, New York, was also interested in using Porsche engines in a single-seat helicopter for the US Navy. Hoffman stopped in Stuttgart while on holiday and helped plan the itinerary, which included a visit to the Studebaker plant in South Bend, Indiana. On this August 1952 trip, Ferry was accompanied by his wife and a contingent of engineers including Karl Rabe on the liner *Queen Elizabeth*—an ocean voyage meant to give everyone an opportunity for a few days of relaxation. The holiday mood ended abruptly, however, with the news of Anton Piëch's death from a heart attack. Unable to return for the funeral, they sailed on toward America and the opportunities that lay ahead.

Hoffman drove with the group from New York to Indiana where the plans for a new Porsche-designed small car were shown to Studebaker management. Ferry Porsche wrote, "They looked at the drawings and said, 'That's not actually

Competition Motors, Hollywood, 1950s
Johnny von Neumann opened a shop in North Hollywood in 1948, catering to the small but growing group of sports car enthusiasts. By the mid 1950s, he was a full-fledged Porsche dealer and the name Competition Motors was appropriate, even if it was displayed under a VW logo. A short distance away was Mulholland Drive, a ribbon of road that wound along the hilltops above Hollywood. Famous among sightseers and hot rodders alike, it was the perfect place to demonstrate the superiority of a light, agile and well-built car like the Porsche. Porsche

A Hoffman ad promoting the "amazing new" 1952 Porsches.

51

what we had in mind, because we did not want to depart from our normal styling'!"

A prototype Porsche four-seater, the Type 530 coupe brought from Germany was demonstrated to the Studebaker people and Hoffman recalls that the car, with four people inside, "thumped like a machine gun" on a rough road. An agreement was reached, however, and the American company signed a contract for development of a new small car. Studebaker was showing some signs of progressive thinking, such as its new Raymond Loewy-designed models, but the company was mired in a bog of financial difficulties. The project continued for some time and Porsche produced two interesting prototypes, Type 542. By 1954, however, the handwriting was on the wall and as Studebaker merged with Packard, the

A four-seater coupe, called the Type 530, was pursued to the prototype stage in 1952, and this cabriolet came later. Compared to the standard 356, the Type 530 had a longer door and extended wheelbase. Note the lengthened area between the door and torsion bar cover and the rolldown rear window. The dashboard was a styling exercise dating from the Studebaker contract days. Road & Track

Porsche design was quietly shelved. The car was never built, but something more important was: a new Porsche factory that was financed chiefly through design fees from Studebaker.

During the 1952 trip, Max Hoffman exerted other influences that were directly related to the future of Porsche cars. He suggested that an emblem would be an image-builder in the American market. Ferry Porsche sketched out a heraldic design on a luncheon napkin using the crest of the house of Württemburg with stag horns and horizontal stripes, the coat of arms of the city of Stuttgart with its prancing horse and displaying the name Porsche prominently above. The drawing was finalized by Komenda and the design department with help from Erich Strenger, who had begun producing sales brochures for Porsche in 1951 and would create much of the literature and many famous posters in the years to come. Yet another suggestion that had far-reaching effects was made by Hoffman: a sporty, simple and most importantly, inexpensive convertible for American boy-racers. It's probable that Hoffman even thought of the name: Speedster.

Hoffman was a combination of flamboyant showman and canny entrepeneur, and he did things with style—as his New York showrooms demonstrated. In addition to the Park Avenue agency, Frank Lloyd Wright designed a house for him near Rye, New York. And it wasn't until the third try that Wright was able to satisfy him—Hoffman had a way of getting just what he wanted. His enthusiasm for driving extended beyond the racetrack, and Wright's memories of Hoffman include hair-raising rides to the building site in his "little Porsche sports car."

Max Hoffman was instrumental in bringing success to Porsche in America and he did the same for Jaguar, Mercedes-Benz, Alfa Romeo, BMW and a host of other European marques. His suggestions led to the Mercedes 190SL, BMW 507, Alfa Romeo Giulietta spider and, of course, the Porsche American Roadster and Speedster. In 1952, Ferry Porsche presented him with a miniature silver coupe in honor of his racing efforts that year, when he had won almost a dozen East Coast events. Hoffman's direct involvement as a Porsche importer lasted until 1964 when Porsche set up its own distribution system, but he will be remembered as one of the most influential automotive figures in the postwar decades.

The English Market

Porsche's entry into England was a long and tortuous affair beginning in 1951 at the Earl's Court Motor Exhibition in London. Britain was closed to auto imports until 1953, and a

One of Max Hoffman's early ads announcing the Porsche "jewels."

Porsche engines were also sold for aeronautical use. In this application, the Gyrodyne corporation of New York used a vertically-mounted engine in a one-man observation platform for the US Marine Corps. Porsche

general feeling of animosity overshadowed commercial exchange with Germany, so special permits had to be obtained to even allow the three cars that were shown into the country.

Charles Meisl, a transplanted Czech, was the driving force behind the introduction of the marque in England. He had seen the cars at the 1950 Geneva Auto Show, and from his position as a salesman with Connaught Cars in Surrey was able to get that company to sponsor the importation of two Porsches to be shown at Earl's Court and a third for demonstration purposes. Meisl was a believer, and when Connaught wouldn't pursue an agency agreement with Porsche, he moved down the road to John Colborne-Baber's VW garage—even British soldiers were bringing the "beetle cars" home from Germany—and found a more receptive attitude toward the new sports cars.

Another member of the English car trade, Bill Aldington, had also taken note of the 1950 Geneva display and the favorable press that Porsche had been receiving. He and his brothers Harold ("Aldy") and Donald were the proprietors of AFN, Ltd., with headquarters in Isleworth, Middlesex. The company was an outgrowth of Archie Frazer-Nash's car-building enterprise and had enjoyed a good deal of success importing BMWs before the war, under the name Frazer-Nash-BMW. In 1950, the brothers were struggling to reestablish themselves, but after an aborted joint venture with the Bristol Aircraft Company, they had produced only a handful of cars.

Hoffmann, New York, 1950s
Max Hoffman's connections in Germany went beyond Stuttgart. When Porsche began to build its own USA distribution network in 1959, Hoffman changed his focus to the BMW marque. By the 1970s he had established the Bavarian carmaker as a force in the American market. Porsche

After the Porsches were shown at Earl's Court, Bill Aldington was able to convince his brother Aldy that these cars were what AFN's customers wanted. Aldy went to Stuttgart and met with an old friend from the BMW racing days before the war, Baron Huschke von Hanstein, now the Porsche racing and public relations manager. He was introduced to Prinzing, the finance chief, who explained that Meisl held the English agency rights. Determined to persuade Porsche management that AFN was the group best suited for an import license, Aldy suggested that Meisl come to his company as sales manager. Porsche and Meisl were both amenable to the idea, and late in 1953, the first Stuttgart car, cabriolet serial number 60277, arrived at AFN's Falcon Works. The first sale was made in January 1954, but it took another four months for the second. In the next few years, as the Porsche business increased, AFN slowly relinquished other pursuits, including motorcycles and sidecars, BMW Isettas, DKWs and even the last of the autos bearing its own Frazer-Nash nameplate.

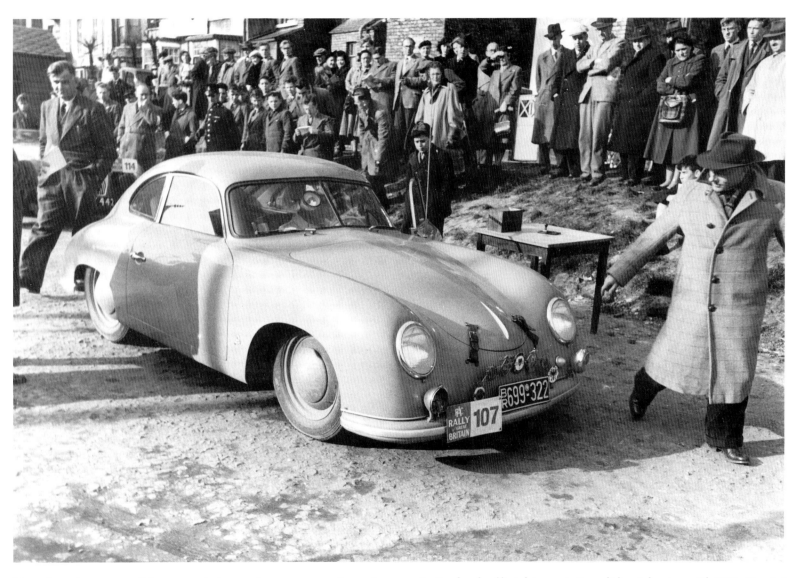

Most Porsche owners did not use their cars for transportation only. Speed trials and rallys like this Royal Automobile Club event in 1952 brought out many private entries. This was one of the first Porsches in England; official importation did not begin until 1953. Road & Track

Le Mans, 1952
Returning to Le Mans in 1952 as reigning champion in its class, the factory again entered two modified Gmünd coupes, one driven by Petermax Müller and Huschke von Hanstein, the other shared by Veuillet/Mouche who would reprise as 1100 cc class winners. A third, private entry in the 1500 cc class was disqualified during the race. Tom Countryman

Chapter 6

Racing, Records and Rallys

From Le Mans to the Carrera Panamericana

Production at the Stuttgart factory quickly built momentum. On March 21, 1951, the 500th German-built Porsche rolled off the line with a garland of greens on its nose. In April, the Porsche display at the Frankfurt Auto Show was chosen as the venue for introducing a number of improvements. In the newest cars, defrosting and ventilation were improved, and tubular rear shocks gave the rear end a more stable attitude in cornering. Alfred Teves' firm, Ate, was now willing to supply

Del Mar, California, May 1960
The first of the cars from Gmünd and Zuffenhausen were not designed as competition vehicles, but it was not long before they were put to that use. By the late 1950s, racetracks in Europe and the United States were filled with 356 coupes and roadsters. Here at Del Mar, a lone MGA rounds the bales surrounded by a quintet of Porsches driven by Ed Barker in the lead, R.G. Kirby, G. Beitel, H. Montonen and F. Man. Dave Friedman

the twin-leading-shoe front brakes. These brakes were a necessary advancement since the engineers were ready to unveil their new engine—the 1300.

The new powerplant, Type 506, was still in essence the VW engine case and crankshaft with a stroke of 64 mm. The

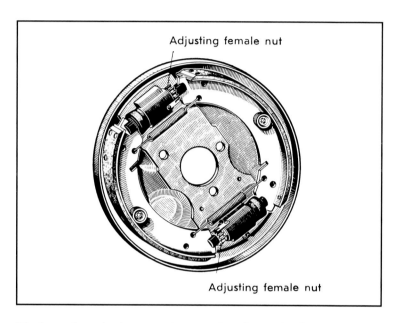

The front drum brakes were improved with twin leading shoes, each one having its own wheel cylinder. Tubular shocks at the rear helped as well. Porsche

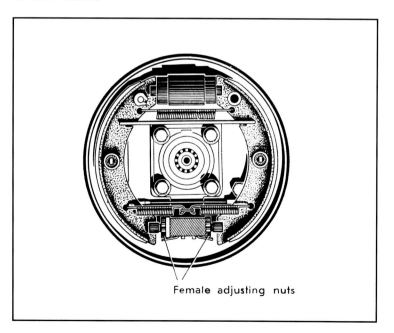

displacement increase came about by increasing the bore to 80 mm and a piston with a dome offset to the intake side to increase combustion efficiency. The cylinders themselves were the result of years of development by the Mahle company which was able to chrome plate the inside surface of the aluminum-finned barrels. Pinholes across the chrome bores allowed oil droplets to adhere to the smooth surface for ring lubrication. This new design allowed better heat dissipation, a rate of thermal expansion that more closely matched the rest of the engine and a weight savings of 12 lb. per engine. The engine was also relatively quiet, and could produce 44 hp at 4200 rpm with a compression ratio of 6.5:1—a figure more compatible with fuels of the day.

The new engine proved its ability in the Baden-Baden Rally that June. Flat-out stages on the open autobahn were run by three coupes, both factory and privateers, averaging 75 mph. Using special factory test license plates that allowed the cars to exceed the 50 mph speed limit, they ran flawlessly for thirty hours. The 1300 soon became a best seller in the model line, with more than 900 built in 1951.

From the first, Porsche cars were being brought into the competition arena by private owners. The 1100 cc class wins came in the Swedish Midnight Sun Rally in 1950 and 1951, along with numerous other victories in local events. The factory gave them as much support as possible, but their own fledgling racing efforts were putting a strain on the company's

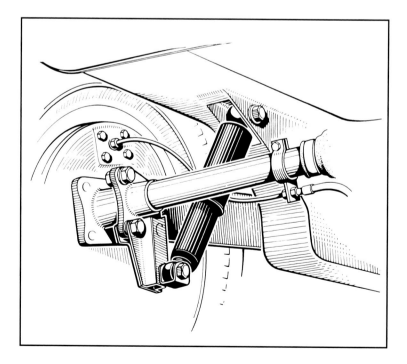

space and manpower, which was already working full bore just to fill the orders for new automobiles.

The Porsche automobile was based on the Volkswagen out of necessity, but this very heritage was the greatest obstacle to its ever becoming a racing machine, in spite of the early successes. The designers were well aware of these inherent limitations and on the drawing boards was a totally new powerplant—a multi-cam unit designed for the racetrack. But in the meantime, a new 1500 cc engine was ready to give customers what they had been clamoring for—more horsepower.

The move to a larger displacement was a logical step for Porsche. In an automobile of the weight and dimensions of the 356, an engine of around 1.0 liter was sufficient to simply propel the car, but it left little margin for performance. The cylinder walls of the 1300 were already pushed out as far as they could be, so a lengthened stroke was the only way to get

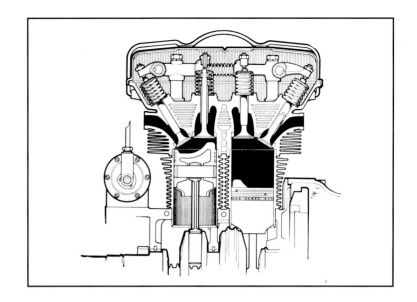

Oil Cleaning

In addition to the oil-strainer, a permanently magnetized filter is located at the opening of the oil-pump intake. This filters out those tiny metal particles, and other foreign matter, which might otherwise damage the gears or engine bearings.

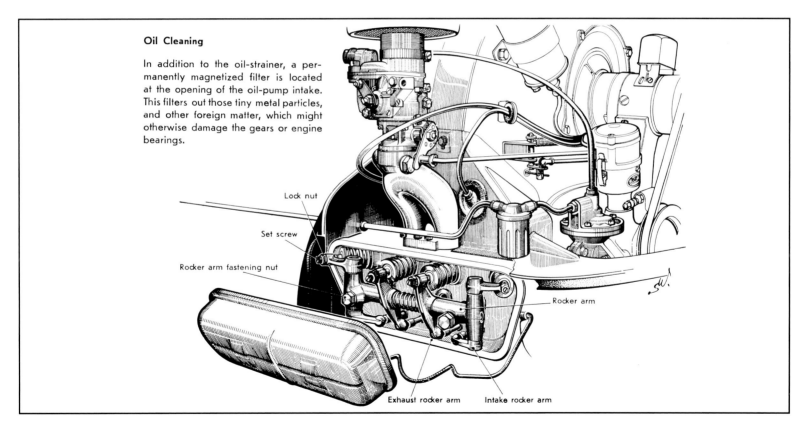

Lock nut

Set screw

Rocker arm fastening nut

Rocker arm

Exhaust rocker arm   Intake rocker arm

The angled exhaust valves were the primary difference between the Porsche head and the VW from which it derived. The 1300 and 1500 Damen engines had short cast manifolds carrying smaller carbs. On 1953 models the valve adjusting screws were moved to the pushrod end of the rocker arm. Pistons in the 1300 were shaped with a crown toward the intake valve, forming a compact charge near the spark plug. Porsche

more displacement. There was a small problem, though: a longer throw would put the crankshaft into an orbit that overlapped with the cam just below it in the crankcase. The big-end bolt bosses that protruded from the connecting rods were the culprits, but the question was how to make these bolts smaller and still safely hold the two rod halves together. The answer was simple: do away with the bolts altogether, using a one-piece rod with smooth shoulders. The actual application of this idea was considerably more involved, though, and required a crankshaft that could be assembled from pieces. Conveniently, the technology and production capacity for such a unit were right in Porsche's backyard, at the Albert Hirth company. This Stuttgart firm had worked with Porsche on the Cisitalia project of 1947 and had considerable experience in the field. Hirth was engaged by Porsche to manufacture the components and assemble crankshafts as well as deal with rebuilds and repairs. This association would last almost a decade and a half—longer, even, than the Hirth company itself would survive.

While the primary consideration for adopting the roller-bearing crank was to gain clearance for added stroke, it also benefited from lower friction at high rpm but conversely, would not tolerate lugging at low speeds. Other drawbacks to this approach were higher initial costs and a somewhat abbreviated lifespan unless the engine was treated properly with clean oil, proper warm-up and correct tuning. At the

A 1950 cabriolet interior shows the deluxe horn ring, optional tachometer, radio and a distinctive horn button, which, like the mirror light and tinted visors, were a means of expressing individuality—as though owning a Porsche in 1950 was not rare enough.

time, it was the only way for Porsche to produce a 1.5 liter engine.

The result was the Type 502: 1488 cc with a stroke of 74 mm (up from 64 mm in the VW) and a bore of 80 mm using the Mahle aluminum and chrome cylinders. The first engines, made available to customers in fall 1951, had a 7.0:1 compression ratio and were fitted with Solex 32 PBI downdraft carburetors producing 55 hp at 4500 rpm. Karl Ludvigsen, in *Porsche: Excellence Was Expected,* stated that only sixty-six of these engines were built.

Type 502 was soon replaced by the Type 527, which used 40 PBIC carbs and added 5 hp at 5000 rpm. With the versatile PBI carburetor series, one could swap throttle bodies and with the 527 engine, the factory offered both the 40 and 32 models with 24, 26 or even 29 mm throats for racing.

The Long Road to the Longest Day

By late winter 1950, preparations were already being made for that monster of endurance racing, Le Mans. It would be an opportunity for considerable exposure, but the cost and logistical problems were a real concern and a poor finish would probably have negative effects on the reputation that the company was slowly building. An added complication was the concern over anti-German sentiment that still ran high in parts of France. For a twenty-four-hour race, Ferry Porsche was stretching the company's capabilities, but his father had believed it could be done, and this first factory racing effort laid the groundwork for a developing Porsche philosophy, which he stated in his book, *We at Porsche:* "Journalists' reports of races are far more effective and convincing than most forms of advertising, and they cost little or nothing. Money thus freed from unnecessary advertising can be used to gain valuable racing experience, and the lessons so learned mean that next year's model can be a better car."

Chosen for battle were three aluminum Gmünd coupes, lighter and more aerodynamic than their steel Stuttgart siblings. We can also assume that these "leftover" cars were more expendable than the "new" German model. With 46 hp and higher gears they could just top 100 mph. The additional power came from a new camshaft designed by a young engineer named Ernst Fuhrmann. Officially, these were 1400 lb. prototypes with numerous body modifications and larger fuel tank with external filler. The factory published a brochure offering these options on what they called the 356 SL, but such a car existed only on paper, solely to validate its entry in the race.

Early on, the effort seemed star-crossed when one of the cars was damaged in an effort to avoid a bicycle on the circuit during practice. Another was thoroughly trashed in an auto-

bahn collision, although the mechanic driving escaped serious injury. The salvageable parts of these two cars were combined together and another Gmünd coupe was quickly drafted into service as a racer. But a team of two cars was just not in the cards for Porsche that year; one of the remaining pair was destroyed in practice during a rainstorm. The hopes of the team were now invested in a single car driven by Auguste Veuillet, who had originally suggested Porsche's effort, and another Frenchman, Edmond Mouche. Ferry Porsche spent the entire race in the pits with his crew and at the checkered flag, their car had won the 1100 cc class and placed twentieth overall with an average speed of just more than 73 mph.

The June 1951 event in France was followed by a mid-August entry in the Liège-Rome-Liège Rally. Two cars were sent to compete in this grueling marathon through the mountains, aluminum Gmünd coupes once again. Covering more than 3,000 miles of roads of all description, the cars were pummeled over narrow mountain passes where both climbing ability and braking power were important. One of these was outfitted with an 1100 cc engine with power output now pushed to 51 hp using gasoline. Driving was shared by Peter-max Müller and Huschke von Hanstein, who in the next year

Montlhéry, 1951
The Gmünd coupe makes a pit stop during its record-setting attempt. In spite of a failing transmission and a refueling snafu, the car broke ten records and was taken directly to the Paris Auto Show, bugs, dirt and all. Porsche

would be hired by Porsche and later become racing director. They brought the car to the finish line second in class. The other Porsche, driven by Paul Guilleaume and Count von der Mühle, was said to have a 1300 cc engine, but aroused curiosity among those looking on. It neither sounded nor performed like its sibling and in fact, finished third overall and first in the 1500 cc class despite transmission problems. It was indeed a 1.5 liter engine, but one more trial by fire awaited before it would be officially announced.

Petermax Müller had set international speed and distance records with his VW-based home-builts in 1950 at the Montlhéry track outside Paris and now he urged Porsche to do the same with their cars. Veuillet had demonstrated two cars to the press in March at this same 1½ mile banked track, promoting both the marque and his company, Sonauto, as French agent for Porsche. In preparation for their attempt, the factory "racing department," a small corner of the Reutter space, readied two cars, 1.1 and 1.5 liter aluminum coupes fitted with flush skirts over the wheels. Along with Müller, other drivers were to be von Hanstein, Richard von Frankenberg, Hermann Ramelow and Walter Glöckler, who also brought a roadster of his own. Ferry Porsche, numerous factory mechanics and a bevy of curious onlookers set up camp at Montlhéry in the last week of September 1951. The 1100 cc car began a run that set new records for 500 miles, 1,000 kilometers and six hours, each at just more than 100 mph. Glöckler's roadster also set three short-distance records for 1500 cc cars and posted a fastest lap of more than 120 mph.

The next day, September 30, the 1500 cc car began a three-day enduro intended to supercede the existing absolute mark of just more than 80 mph for seventy-two hours, this set some sixteen years earlier by a 3.0 liter Citröen. After two days, the car was averaging about 99 mph and a number of 1500 cc class records were secured. The final goal, still almost a day away, seemed within reach until a routine refueling stop went awry. The fuel filler, back under the hood for aerodynamic reasons, was opened as the car stopped and the mechanics were ready with the fuel hose, but no gas flowed when the valve was opened. In a confused scramble, the men tried to find the problem, but precious moments were slipping by. An onlooker, a Porsche customer from Germany, ran to his car and the gas can he kept there. The few gallons from his can were enough to get the silver coupe back on track while the faulty valve was found and repaired.

But the ordeal was not over. In the small hours of the final morning, the monotonous sound of the circling car suddenly ended when it rolled into the pits with a broken transmission. The mechanics struggled with the non-synchro gearbox, desperately trying to get the car back on the track. After some ten

minutes they were able to engage third gear, but no other. A quick calculation showed that a new record could still be had, at increased engine revs—if the engine would last. Pushing it back on the track, the group waited tensely through the night, but the car survived and at the end of its run had amassed ten new class records in addition to the absolute seventy-two-hour speed mark.

The new record would last only a year, but for that time it was a promotional opportunity that Porsche was quick to pursue. Taken directly to Paris for the opening of the 1951 auto show, the car still wore a coating of dirt and oil from its record run. Bloody but unbowed, it joined a Stuttgart-built car on the Porsche stand and attracted curious crowds and the attention of automotive writers who were quick to accomplish what Porsche had set out to do—boost the image of the company and the sale of cars.

Filling the Trophy Case

"Competition improves the breed" is a phrase well known to automotive engineers, but it was especially taken to heart by those in Zuffenhausen. The Porsche name itself was steeped in racing tradition and the first advertising brochures had made pointed reference to the old professor and his high-performance creations, especially the Auto Union cars of the 1930s. But the company could no longer rest on twenty-year-old laurels.

Enthusiastic customers were successfully campaigning Porsches in production car racing classes, a new type of race program developing in Germany at the time. Private entrants could pit their cars and skill against others in a series-built production class race, essentially a stock car contest, usually presented as an adjunct to a motorcycle or sports car race and often on famous circuits like the Nürburgring. At the same time, the American armed forces became benefactors of the sports car crowd when airfields began to be opened on weekends for semi-formal meets. The flat and wide courses were especially popular among novices, whose only danger in a spin was a smashed hay bale or a bruised ego. It was not Grand Prix racing, although the combination of overzealous drivers and tail-happy cars gave the spectators a good show.

Denis Jenkinson, an English journalist and early devotee of Porsche cars, described the proper driving method: "The works Porsche drivers developed a particular skill which counteracted this [oversteer], in which they deliberately provoked the oversteer with the steering wheel, instantly unwinding it and equally as quickly winding it on again.... going into a long fast bend you set up a 'sawing' motion on the wheel to coincide with the yawing action of the car, and this resulted in reasonable stability at quite high cornering powers." The technique came to be known as *wischen* and *sagen*, literally meaning "wiping" and "sawing." Jenkinson also noted, "If you got out of step in the motion the car would do a flick-roll onto its roof!"

The privateers were having a good time, but the real focus of public attention was on races like Le Mans, the Mille Miglia and the Marathon of the Road—the Liège-Rome-Liège Rally. For this 1952 event, a 1500 cc aluminum coupe was entered by the factory and won outright at the hands of Helmut Polensky and Walter Schlüter. Private entrants swelled the ranks of 1500 cc Porsches in the first ten places: third, fourth, ninth and tenth overall. The victory was complete and the accolades numerous, but the year had just begun.

In May there was again a single works entry for the Mille Miglia Grand Touring class: the aluminum coupe, now pro-ducing about 70 hp. Driving was shared by two titled gentle-men, Counts Lurani and Konstantin Berckheim, who managed a class win in spite of having to finish the race in third gear. Privateer entries included a 1500 and two 1100 cc cars, one of the latter, driven by Prince Metternich and Count Einseidel, also taking class honors. In the other 1.5 liter car, Helmut Polensky, a German, misunderstood his Italian co-driver's directions given in French just before a curve. The car rolled, becoming a bit more compact in the process. While still driv-able, there was no way to sit upright inside. One of the locals swarming around the site was a large man, the local butcher, who took it upon himself to climb inside and with his back, push the roof up in place. Returning to the road with goggles, the pair valiantly made up time until they had to retire with engine trouble.

Lake Phalen, Minnesota, 1954
From the beginning, Porsche drivers made their mark in hillclimbs, rallys and ice races. One-armed Otto Mathé campaigned his Gmünd coupe on the frozen lakes of Europe, and it was not long before Americans discovered the handling and traction advantages of a rear-engine car. Tom Countryman entered his 1951 1300 coupe in the Lake Phalen ice race in St. Paul, Minnesota. This race in early 1954 gave most local spectators their first view of a Porsche and for the other competitors on the sanded ice track, the view was mostly of the coupe's tail. Countryman won the race handily against MGs and assorted other front-engine sports cars. Ice racing demanded special skills and special equipment like the front and rear bumper bars, frost panels on the windows and an army tank commander's helmet. Note the new-style slotted rear wheels and the tripod-mounted cock-pit camera. The same car was on the grid of the first race held at Elkhart Lake in Wisconsin the next year. By that time, starting grids at racetracks across the country were filled with Porsches. Tom Countryman

The next month Porsche returned to their race headquarters in the French village of Tèloché with two 1100 cc aluminum Gmünd coupes. Veuillet and Mouche, Le Mans class winners the previous year, were joined by Petermax Müller and von Hanstein. The latter team had an early lead but was forced to drop out, and Veuillet and Mouche were again victors in the 1.1 category. A third, privately entered car of 1.5 liters was well placed in the race, but fell victim to a controversial disqualification. Le Mans rules stated that the motor must be turned off during driver changes, but apparently the

engine ran on for a few seconds, technically putting the team out of contention. The Gmünd coupes, which had begun their careers as road cars, had done yeoman service in competition, but this was their last factory appearance in a major race.

Carrera Panamericana 1952

November 1952 saw the entry of two Porsches in another type of contest, this time on the American continent. The Carrera Panamericana road race in Mexico was in its third year, run along almost 2,000 miles of the new Pan American

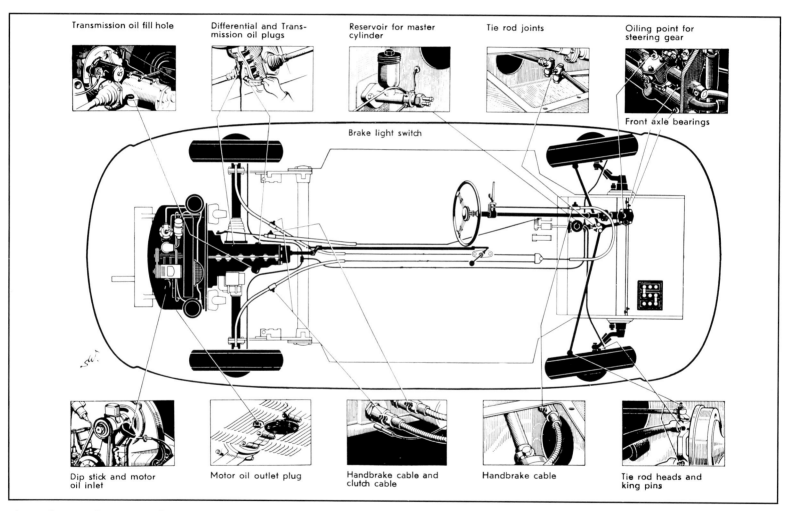

Transmission oil fill hole Differential and Transmission oil plugs Reservoir for master cylinder Tie rod joints Oiling point for steering gear

Brake light switch Front axle bearings

Dip stick and motor oil inlet Motor oil outlet plug Handbrake cable and clutch cable Handbrake cable Tie rod heads and king pins

The early Porsches required a certain amount of maintenance, and the owner's manual gave instructions for everything short of a teardown. While European owners were often wealthy or titled men, American enthusiasts tended to be engineers or technically oriented people who appreciated the finely-crafted qualities of the car and often performed their own repairs. Porsche Panorama, the magazine

of the Porsche Club of America, regularly carried articles examining the merits of new products, new mechanical techniques and helpful hints, ranging from where to cut a hole in the dash for your radio to the effectiveness of diatomaceous earth as an oil-filtering medium. Porsche

Highway starting in the south at Tuxtla Gutiérrez and ending near the American border at Ciudad Juárez. It was a test of speed and endurance over surfaces that sometimes only marginally fit the definition of a "road" with overall elevation changes of 10,000 ft. Large American cars took to the environment quite well, and the field this year featured a mixed bag of machinery from Mercurys to Ferraris, as well as Mercedes' new 300SL, the eventual winner.

Carrera Panamericana, 1953
After a modest but respectable showing in the 1952 Carrera, Porsche coupes and Spyders both took part the following year. Fernando Segura's shiny 356 did not stay that way for long. He drove a consistent race and finished second in class to José Herrarte's Spyder in 1953. Here Herbert Linge, left, and Juroslav Juhan are either choosing carburetor jets or having a snack. Dave Friedman

The little Porsche coupes seemed almost too fragile for this kind of adventure, but their diminutive size made them a favorite with the locals, who referred to Paul von Metternich as, "The Prince who speaks Spanish and drives a toy car." His steel-bodied 1500 Super cabriolet finished eighth overall after four days and numerous complications, including an overnight valve job by factory mechanic Herbert Linge. Another 356, a steel coupe, was driven by young Count Konstantin "Tin" von Berckheim, with Linge in the passenger seat. On the third leg, so the story went, a rock broke the transmission case, putting them out of the contest. Years later it was admitted that the so-called rock came from inside the case—it was in fact an early synchro transmission that had failed.

Both Porsches had been imported to Mexico by Prince Alfons von Hohenlohe who during the race took full advantage of the little cars' curiosity value. He got the cars and drivers on four separate television programs, one of which was sponsored by General Motors. Though other factories had sent complete teams, both of the 356s entered were shoestring operations. The Porsche spares were considerately carried from checkpoint to checkpoint by the Mercedes crews, and at one point, a penniless von Metternich even had to borrow a tank of fuel. It was an inauspicious beginning, but in the next few years Porsche would take from the event not only class honors, but a name synonymous with high-performance racing.

Carrera Panamericana, 1953
English actress Jaqueline Evans entered all five of the Carreras, in 1953 switching from an American sedan to this 356, curiously decorated in memory of Eva Peron. She was eliminated on the first leg after having reached the finish five minutes over the alotted time. For 1954 she was back in an ex-Rome-Liégé-Rome aluminum Gmünd coupe, probably the last time one of the original Porsche competition models was seen in an international race. Dave Friedman

Chapter 7

Improving the Breed

New Cars, New Buildings, New Horizons

During the winter of 1951–1952, the engine designers were not the only busy people in the Porsche "design studio," the drafty wooden barracks just south of the original Porsche works. Erwin Komenda was making changes to the chassis and body that would ease construction and improve both the utilitarian and aesthetic appeal of the car. The rate of change was fast and furious during 1952 and improvements were phased in as soon as possible, an attitude that would

The 1953 models carried the Porsche crest on the steering wheel hub. Ventilated wheels and dual-outlet exhaust were also new. Porsche

distinguish the company from its American counterparts whose cars were often a tribute to form over substance.

In 1951, new oval vents on the disc wheels helped cool the brakes and later, aluminum "turbo" slotted trim rings made an appearance as an option. The two-piece windshield, a concession to the economics of low-volume production, was replaced in mid 1952 by a single, bent glass, curved slightly at its outer edges. In the months preceding the fall introduction of the

1953 models, a number of other body changes were made including bumpers that were mounted on spring plates and projected out from the body, which now curved down and in at its lower edges.

Up until this time, the phrase trunk space was an oxymoron, but moving the spare to a more vertical position allowed a bit more luggage to be taken along, since there was now a folding seat in the rear area. Cabriolet tops had previously included a glass rear window in a wooden frame on the Reutter bodies or an aluminum frame in the bodies being built for Porsche by Heuer. Each was changed to a larger, clear plastic piece for the 1953 cars. The rectangular taillight was dropped and became one of two round beehive lenses on each side, joining a small glass reflector just above the bumper. The center license and stoplight now became a license and back-up light just above the license area and the front running lights moved outward, under the headlights. Inside, the gauges, now black and green, received visors for better visibility and a tachometer became standard equipment, replacing the usual clock. A column-mounted switch controlled the turn signals, replacing a dash toggle. New owners didn't have to carry spare throttle cables anymore as the cable was replaced by a rod.

The 1500, now a year old, had become a favorite among the journalist ranks, and judging by sales, also with the customers. The demand was such that in October 1952, Porsche announced two new versions of the larger engine. Superseding the 527, the new Type 528 carried on with a roller-bearing crankshaft, but in addition, the camshaft was reconfigured for 1 mm higher lift and considerably more duration. Compression was up to 8.2:1 and of course, the larger 40 PBIC carburetors were used with long, welded steel manifolds. These fed the cylinders through larger ports and special valve springs. Exhaust valves were sodium filled for cooling and a larger, double-outlet muffler also helped breathing. Now called the 1500S or Super, horsepower was up to 70 at 5400 rpm with 80 lb-ft of torque at 3600. Patterned after the Montlhéry record car engine, its power band was heavily weighted at the top end; in the lower revs its sibling, the Type 546, could pull harder.

For the more reserved driver, the 1500 Normal, or *Dame* as it became known, was the engine of choice. In the time since the roller crank appeared, Karl Rabe had found another way to solve the clearance problem: by cutting the outer corners off the lower rod half. In its final form, the bottom half of the rod was a smooth crescent with the threaded studs an integral part. This Type 546 was a shell-bearing version of the 527 engine, but with a mild cam, smaller carbs and a 7.0:1 compression ratio. It was tuned to produce a smooth 55 hp at 4400 rpm. The two other engines, 1100 and 1300 cc, were continued,

Paris Auto Show, 1953
The autumn 1953 show introduced the new 550 Spyder to the public. Also on display was the synchromesh transmission and for American military and civilian buyers, whitewall tires and credit at six percent. Porsche

but with improvements. All the engines now had rocker arms with adjusting screws at the pushrod end.

These advances in engine design were important, but of marginal value unless the rest of the car could work in harmony with the increased power. The VW brakes, which had long been recognized as a weak point, were upgraded with a new design that came on-line in August 1952. The new drums, 280 mm in diameter and 40 mm wide, increased swept area by forty percent at all four corners. Unsprung weight was decreased by casting the new finned drum from aluminum, with steel liners for the shoe contact area and bearing race.

Porsche Type 519 Synchronized Gearbox

One other problem area remained. The original VW gearbox, when used in competition, had been consistent in one regard—it always failed when pushed to the limit. A new

The 1500 S engine came on line in late 1952. Shown here sans cooling shrouds, the larger Solex carbs and welded manifolds with balance tube are visible. The lateral rod linkage was affected by temperature changes and replaced with pivot arms a few years later. Porsche

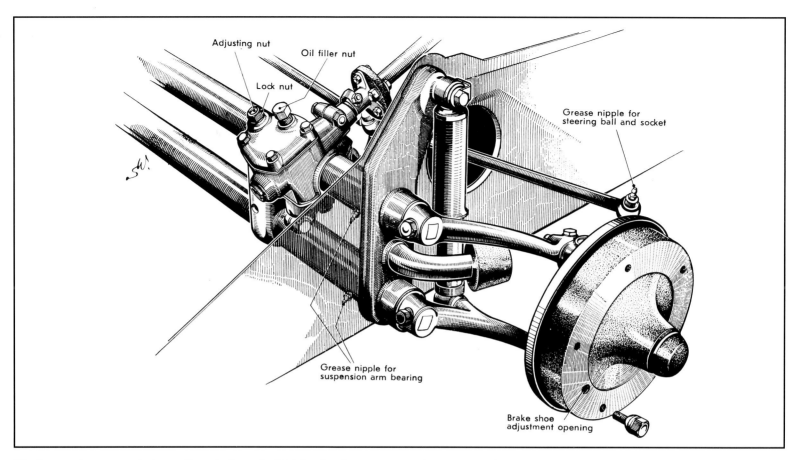

Adjusting nut

Oil filler nut

Lock nut

Grease nipple for
steering ball and socket

Grease nipple for
suspension arm bearing

Brake shoe
adjustment opening

The front axle was carried over directly from the VW, but by the 1952 models twin-leading-shoe Lockheed brakes were fitted, with finned aluminum and iron drums. King pins and link pins were retained throughout the life of the 356 line. Porsche

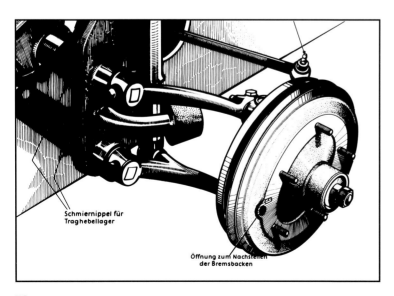

Schmiernippel für
Traghebellager

Öffnung zum Nachstellen
der Bremsbacken

transmission, the Type 519, finally went into production in summer 1952, after a long and circuitous development route that began five years before. Split-ring sychronizers, the basic concept that would become the heart of the new design, first appeared on drawings for the Cisitalia five-speed transmission. Leopold Schmid was a specialist in transmissions and drivetrains. He was two years younger than Ferry Porsche, and had come to work for the Porsche design firm in 1941, remaining with the refugee firm in Gmünd. Part of his design for the Italian Grand Prix car transmission was a system of split rings—collars that would ease the engagement, up or down, of each gear. In the new Porsche transmission, the system brought each respective mainshaft and countershaft gear to the same speed so their teeth could easily mesh.

The whole design exercise was intended as a sales pitch to Volkswagen; they needed a synchronized transmission, and if VW built it, Porsche would be more than happy to buy the units from them. Schmid was able to fit the new gears and synchro rings into the VW split-case without undue difficulty, but convincing Wolfsburg was another matter. Heinz Nordhoff and his new chief engineer, both former Opel men, decided instead to use a Borg-Warner device that they were familiar with. So if Porsche wanted to use their own new design, they would have to find a supplier with the ability and experience to build the transaxles for them. The task was given to the Getrag company, probably only because they were close to Zuffenhausen, since their expertise was in heavy equipment transmissions. The first units from Getrag had all the smoothness of a tractor gearbox, so testing and assembly were moved to Zuffenhausen. The *Windhund* and *Ferdinand* were fitted with 1500 cc engines and the new synchro box, and 50,000 miles later the combination had proven itself.

The split-ring system had advantages not only over the previous Porsche-designed VW transmission, but over other types of synchronizers as well. It was compact, quiet, durable and eminently adaptable, and the company was quick to put

this flexibility to use in the 356. Unchained from the VW crash-box, they could easily change gear ratios for different engines and applications. The 1953 models enjoyed closer spacing in their first three gears with an overall slightly lower numerical ratio. Later transmissions would be available with a choice of three or more ratios for each forward gear, designated by the letters A through E. In addition, two or three final-drive ratios would be available with most units. Albert Prinzing saw these as marketable advantages, and he lost no time in promoting the design to others. Today, after four decades, dozens of patents, and millions of automobiles using the Porsche split-ring system, it remains a milestone in the annals of the company and a great step forward for the 356 series.

The New Zuffenhausen Works

Paris had always been the main venue for new offerings from the house of Porsche, going back to the turn of the century. The October 1952 display at the Grand Palais, showcas-

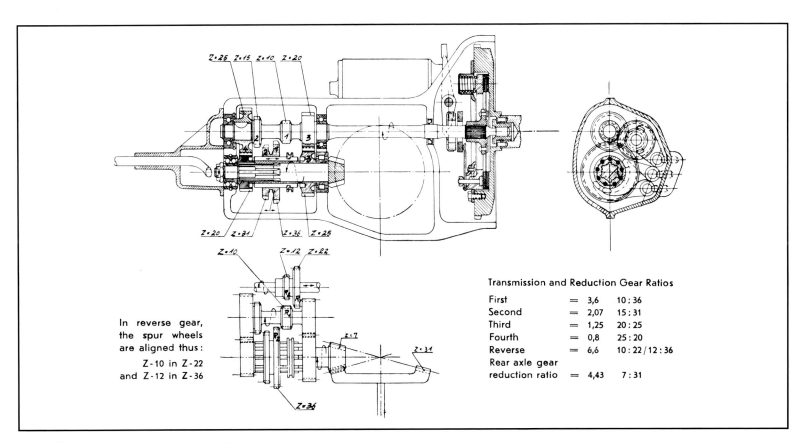

In reverse gear, the spur wheels are aligned thus:
Z-10 in Z-22
and Z-12 in Z-36

Transmission and Reduction Gear Ratios

First	= 3,6	10 : 36
Second	= 2,07	15 : 31
Third	= 1,25	20 : 25
Fourth	= 0,8	25 : 20
Reverse	= 6,6	10 : 22 / 12 : 36
Rear axle gear reduction ratio	= 4,43	7 : 31

The Volkswagen transmission was an ingenious device but was just a bit crude for an expensive car like the Porsche. Porsche

ing the 1953 models with all of these new components, was a watershed event for the company, so recently risen from the ashes of war. The Porsche stand was not extravagant, but it was larger and certainly contained more to interest the prospective buyer than in the previous two years. With the introduction of the 1953 models, Porsche had made enough improvements to satisfy even their most obstreperous critics.

All of these advances were making the Porsche more attractive to an ever-widening circle of customers, and the idea of adding a four-seater to the line was pursued to the

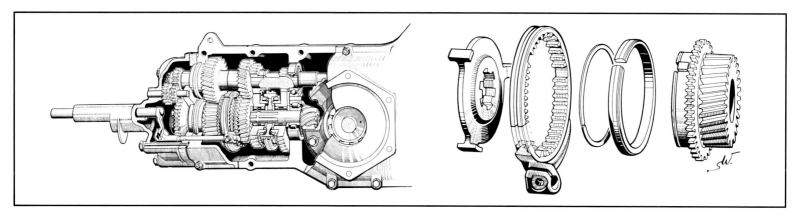

Leopold Schmid's split-ring synchronizers made the new transmission easier to use and tougher for racing applications. Porsche

Hooded instruments were an improvement in the 1953 models, as was the one-piece windshield. A tachometer was now standard.

prototype stage in 1952. Type 530 was built in both coupe and later, cabriolet, versions on a stretched chassis with a 94.5 in. wheelbase. Damen 1.5 liter engines were used in both cars with the new larger brakes and a body with doors and contours to match the extra length. Independent body makers would later continue the four-seater saga but for now, the popularity of the 356 and lack of production capacity precluded its ever joining the Porsche line-up.

In 1950, Stuttgart production had totaled 298 cars, and that number had since doubled, tripled and continued upward. There was no hope of expanding in the present buildings, and the Americans in the original works still gave no indication of when they would leave. The need for a new factory had been obvious since just after the move back to Germany, so in 1951, land behind the Reutter shop in Zuffenhausen was purchased and a building was designed by Rolf Gutbrod, a Stuttgart

Porsche, Zuffenhausen, 1958
The new Porsche Werk II building proudly displays the name of the company. Finished bodies were trucked from the nearby Reutter works, then hoisted onto three-wheeled dollies and wheeled into the assembly area.

architect and professor. But the cost estimates began an upward spiral and the project ground to a halt late in the year.

It was not until May 1952, when the Studebaker development contract was signed, that construction got under way. The building grew, literally, even as it rose: original plans for a single floor of offices were changed to two, then three before construction was complete. Work advanced quickly and from the new Werk II assembly hall, almost 200 ft. long, the first cars rolled out in November. These 1953 models were distinguished by another small but significant detail. The new two-spoke steering wheel carried on its central horn button the Porsche crest. In addition to a thoroughly modern car, the company now had a new factory, a new symbol and what appeared to be a bright future.

America Roadster

The notion of a sports car has always been one in which the design emphasis was placed on those attributes that increase performance, eliminating items that did not. Such mundane appurtenances as rear doors, rear seats and even a top were rejected by purists. In 1950, the well-appointed Porsche convertible fit the description of, and indeed was, a real sports car in comparison with most vehicles on the road,

The America Roadster, the first real sporting roadster on a 356 chassis. Porsche

74

but Porsche knew there was certainly a market for a car that eschewed comfort for capability—a real road-going sports car. As early as 1950 there existed in Stuttgart drawings of a low sport roadster, possibly made at the instigation of Max Hoffman who was personally racing the cars he imported to America, and who had admitted that he thought the 356 body style was awful.

A young businessman in Stuttgart, Heinrich Sauter, had the same idea. He owned a machine tool company, did business with Porsche and raced a Porsche coupe in 1950, but he felt the car was too heavy. Purchasing a chassis from the factory, he had a steel body built at Hans Klenk's shop just outside Stuttgart. Sauter wanted a low, light version of the Porsche cabriolet and had only a few specific requirements—one was that the doors open toward the front to speed in-and-out movement at rally checkpoints. Klenk, who had been a co-driver with Karl Kling in the Carrera Panamericana, was well connected in the automotive city and was regularly in touch with Porsche during construction of the car. The finished car, ready in the spring of 1951, was almost surely the product of a combination of suggestions from Hoffman, as interpreted by Porsche and built by Klenk with input from Sauter.

Under these circumstances, the car could easily have been an ugly bastard, but it actually turned out pretty well. Lower than a standard 356, it had a dropped beltline and widened rear fenders—just the kind of classic touch that Max Hoffman appreciated in the Jaguars he sold. It is thought that the car was used as a first test bed for the new 1500 engine, and was certainly used in testing other items such as rubber-damped wheels. Sauter entered the car in a Nürburgring race in the spring and the Liège-Rome-Liège Rally in August, but completed neither. Sold back to the factory, the roadster was campaigned by François Picard, with more success, in 1952. Back at the factory again, it gathered dust while the Glöckler spiders took the competition limelight. In early 1953 it reached California where Stan Mullin, its new owner, ran a season of races but was already outclassed by newer Porsches. Following a familiar course of neglectful owners, the Sauter car languished until 1982 when it was purchased by Ray Knight who undertook a restoration project of immense proportions, but today the car is close to its original condition. The roadster may have been a one-off, but it had a lot going for it and the Zuffenhausen men didn't waste much time making their own version.

Max Hoffman had seen the Sauter car and expressed approval. By early 1952, Ferry Porsche had placed an order with the Gläser Karosserie firm whose Dresden shops had been moved to Ullersricht, north of Munich, after the war. The proprietor, Georg Heuer, had come to Porsche earlier looking for body-building commissions and was given a contract to produce some of the first cabriolets. Now he was commissioned to produce the aluminum bodies for what would be known as the America Roadster.

Four of the sleek America Roadsters were sent across the Atlantic to the United States in 1952 and about a dozen more the next year. Two series were produced, the second group having double rear grilles for cooling. The cabriolet chassis were trucked to Heuer/Gläser, who welded on the aluminum bodies and sent the assembly back to Zuffenhausen for mechanicals. This cumbersome arrangement partly explains why so few were built, but Gläser was already on the verge of insolvency and the new Spyder was on the way by 1953.

Zuffenhausen, 1952
A rear view of the Sauter car shows the dual-pipe muffler, a distinctive mark of the new 1500 engine. The rally car in the background is testimony to the dangers of racing. The factory was active in support of amateur competitors and regular customers alike. Both racing and road cars were brought to the factory's service department for repair and adjustment. Customers found that along with the requested service, their car was washed and often small trim items were replaced gratis. Tom Countryman

Similar in appearance to the Sauter car, the America was enthusiastically received by influential writers like John Bentley who said, "Correctly driven, it will out-corner and out-brake absolutely anything in the genuine sports car line, any-where near its price." He went on in a 1953 *Auto Age* road test to describe the weight of each removable item, like the wind-screen, top, luggage tray and touring seats and gave details about tuning carbs and selecting plugs. At 1412 lb. fully

Detail changes made in the spring of 1954 included new front grilles for the horns and brake cooling along with windshield washers. The cabriolet featured a fully padded top, plush seating and a choice of engines. In America in 1955 the entire line was called Continental— but not for long. Porsche conceded to Ford's demands and changed the fender script to European, but by 1956 the entire name program was dropped.

stripped, with a 75 hp 1500 cc engine it was a serious competitor and, for a short time, the premier Porsche.

The roadster certainly made a splash in its namesake country, but questions remain to this day about how many were actually built—estimates vary from twelve to 100. For those who were left out, a light and simple street machine would be available a year later, the model that would become arguably the most famous Porsche of all, and it, too, was a Max Hoffman brainchild.

Expansion of the Line

After the many changes leading up to the 1953 Porsches, the production models remained fairly stable during the year. Notable additions include the Type 589, 1300 S engine in November, a blood brother to the 1500 Super, filling the need for a strong engine in the 1.3 liter European racing classes. It used the 74 mm stroke Hirth crank and a hotter cam, and with a 74.5 mm bore could put out 60 hp at 5500 rpm, the highest revving pushrod engine yet. Among the ideas that didn't make production that year was an adaptation of the torsion bar front suspension designed by a young staff engineer named Wolfgang Eyb. With one trailing arm, ball joints and a vertical strut and shock, the unit showed promise but was not used. Another twenty-seven-year-old engineer named Helmuth Bott began working with von Frankenberg on suspension improvements that culminated in the first antiroll bar, installed at the front beginning in November 1954.

At the new Werk II the bodies from Reutter, trucked from across the street, were placed on three-wheeled dollies with a tray underneath that held the mechanical pieces such as suspension and brakes. In 1954, mechanics sat on three-legged stools or rolling creepers to install equipment on the so-called assembly line: some eight cars would be lined up nose-to-tail alongside racks of spare parts. Motors were assembled in a separate area and run on a test stand for at least two hours while power output was checked. Engines of all sizes would generally leave the factory with actual horsepower slightly better than the figures published in sales brochures. DIN (Deutsche Industrie Norm) horsepower figures, which corresponded closely to the actual power available at the rear wheels, were used. This conservative attitude ensured that no new Porsche owner was disappointed after taking delivery. A final sixty-mile test drive on the roads around Stuttgart was made with a canvas cover over the nose of the car. Factory test drivers would surely have smiled to know that their utilitarian "bra" would, thirty years later, become a hot accessory for all kinds of cars, even those which were ill-suited to its use.

In America, the Hoffman-Porsche Car Corporation was taking almost a third of Porsche's 1954 production, but only with 1500 engines. This was, after all, the land of the V-8 and American cars were getting larger and flashier every day. In contrast, the little ladybug-shaped car was a curiosity wherever it appeared, with the exception of the racetrack. But skeptics had only to read any of the numerous road tests appearing in American magazines to realize that this "German automotive jewel" was the kind of thoroughbred that Detroit could only dream about. And as with any jewel, this one had a steep price: $4,284 for the S coupe and $300 more for the cabriolet. For that kind of money, you could see the USA in two Chevrolets and have plenty left over for burgers and chocolate malteds at the new drive-ins along the highway.

Hoffman, consummate salesman that he was, had an answer to the price problem: offer a "stripper" model. The 1500 Normal became the Porsche price leader—named the America and offered without the folding rear seat, wheel trim and radio. Passengers gave up their adjustable seatback and sun visor, but the price was down to $3,445 and only $250 more for the ragtop. Of course, the Porsche convertible was anything but. With roll-up windows and a fully padded and finished folding top, it made most British open cars seem like a joke. And on the track, the open car was as competitive as the coupe, which Art Bunker and Richard Thompson proved by winning the 1954 SCCA F-Production title.

For the first few years, Porsche advertising leaned heavily on the tradition established by the prewar designs of the elder Ferdinand Porsche. But by 1955, with the introduction of the A Series in Sep- tember the 356 was well established as a successful car in its own right.

Chapter 8

The 356 A Series

Building on a Solid Base

In Stuttgart on March 15, 1954, Porsche number 5,000 rolled out the door. As that landmark coupe left the factory, it was Ferry Porsche's hand that guided the car, just as he now guided the fortunes of the company that bore his father's name—and his own. The old professor was not forgotten, however, since it was to a great extent his reputation that had given the fledgling car builder some credence in the marketplace. Journalists writing about the first 356s never failed to mention the elder's exploits, and the public could be forgiven for believing that the senior Ferdinand had actually designed the car—that is how many reporters told the story. Brochures from 1950 showed the 356 with five of Professor Porsche's designs and even in 1953, pointed reference was made in sales literature to the "Prinz Heinrich" and Lohner cars. The press had often referred to the head of the company as "Professor Porsche's son," but by 1954 Ferry's sports car was well known and he was acknowledged as the driving force behind the company. And in addition to creative and management talents, an event that year showed that he had also inherited a bit of the independent spirit from his father.

When Heinz Nordhoff's sales director visited Porsche in 1954 it was with a proposition—to hire Ferry as head of development at VW's Braunschweig research center. There was just one stipulation: that he would give up his Stuttgart business. The offer was lucrative enough, but seemed an attempt to prevent Porsche from designing any successful competitor to the VW. At any rate, Ferry shared his father's feelings about large corporate structures. In *Cars Are My Life* he relates, "My activities as an entrepreneur meant more to me than a position on the board of a large company, where plotting and scheming are an integral part of the job."

The 5,000 car milestone was also poignant to the former Gmünd workers on hand and those who remembered that only four years earlier the first contract for 500 bodies from Reutter seemed like a large risk. In the coming months, running changes and a thorough update to the 356 would increase its appeal so that 5,000 more would be built in the next two years.

The first of these improvements were small front grilles next to the turn signals and more powerful horns mounted behind them. Windshield washers were made standard, along with such interior niceties as a passenger grab bar and coat hooks. In the engine compartment a canister oil filter was mounted to the left of the generator, increasing oil capacity, helping cool the lubricant and offering an improved means of filtering over the simple round strainer at the bottom of the crankcase. And unlike many of the "exotic" items in the engine, the filter elements could be purchased at most auto parts or even tractor parts stores.

Engines for the Future

In late fall 1954 came the introduction, without fanfare, of new and completely revised engines. A larger case, made of aluminum, increased oil capacity by a liter. Now cast in three pieces, the fourth crank bearing rode in a front cover along with distributor and fuel pump drives and the oil pump. Bolted above the third member was the combination generator stand and oil filler-breather. The new case benefited from stronger bearing webs inside and sloping exterior sides that smoothed the exit of warm air from the fan above. Cylinder openings were large enough to accept a planned increase in bore. Other detail changes were a rectangular strainer-drain cover and horizontally machined holes for the new large-head cam followers. At the other end of the pushrod, the valve gear was redesigned to strengthen the intake and exhaust arm, the latter now set at an angle to the rocker shaft. Head and crankcase machining was brought in-house with the installation of several new tools, though Porsche was still dependent on numerous outside suppliers.

In the 356A, the windshield was curved and the dashboard was
redesigned with a padded top that shielded the instruments. Bumper
overriders were popular in the United States.

The new 1300 and 1500 engines, with a Normal and Super in each size, now bore the designation /2 after their type number while the 1100 engine was dropped. Road testers were generally favorable in their reviews, though Denis Jenkinson relates that he received considerable criticism from English counterparts when he bought his own Porsche in 1955. Perhaps one cannot consider Jenkinson a completely objective observer, but his stories do tend to convey the true flavor of Porsche motoring in the 1950s. "I put up with [the criticism] because I thought the aerodynamic shape of the saloon looked about right and it was a car I could lean my elbow on." Jenkinson was known not only for his self-effacing attitude but for his diminutive height and the low coupe was just right for him. He continued, "The whole essence of driving a Porsche lies in the fact that everything is finger-light; the steering, clutch, gear-change and brakes are all of a light smooth feeling that at first comes as strange after conventional cars. It has a live manner in its feeling of going that wants caressing, not taken firmly between clenched fists as on some cars. . . ."

Other writers confirmed Jenkinson's thoughts, but noted that the engines were happiest when driven in the "green stripes"—lines on the tachometer delineating the power band. *The Autocar* stated, "The sports-racing background of the Porsche is discernable from the moment the car moves off." Indeed, as the company embarked on a complete revamping of the 356, advertising made reference to "race tested engineering" and revolved around the phrase, "Years ahead in engineering, miles ahead on the road."

At Frankfurt in September 1955, the new line made its debut with enough changes to warrant a separate designation: 356A. Starting at the bottom, the modifications included 4.5 in. wide rims with 5.60x15 in. tires, found by Helmuth Bott to dramatically improve cornering power though tire manufacturers were concerned over this "ultra wide" wheel. The front steering members were strengthened, the geometry was revised and a damper added. Torsion bars at both ends were softened and larger shocks installed along with a slightly bigger front antiroll bar. A polished aluminum and rubber strip, first seen on the new Speedster, ran along the flatter rocker panel of all the new cars and a new larger handle with the Porsche crest was carried over from the previous year. The bent windshield gave way to curved glass and inside, a new flat dashboard with a padded top featured a large central tach, speedo on the left and combination oil temperature-fuel gauge on the right. Provision was made for a radio in the middle with a passenger grab handle and locking glovebox (except on the Speedster) at right. The clutch cable was moved out from under the driver's foot and with the floorboards gone, an extra 1½ in. of space was available. New self-canceling turn signals,

Rudge knock-off wheels would convince any English skeptic that this was indeed a real sports car. Available through the late 1950s, the Ben Hur style wings on the center knob were not used in Germany, where pedestrian safety precluded any sharp objects on the exterior of a car. Using the same basic drum with a completely different hub assembly, the wheels cost around $600 and did not save any weight, but they did look snazzy.

headlight flasher, handbrake controls and the floor-mounted heater knob from the previous year all made life more pleasant in the cockpit.

The one-year-old 1500 engines were increased in size to 1.6 liters, reflecting the anticipated Federation Internationale de l'Automobile (FIA) class limit change for touring cars. New designations, Types 616/1 and 616/2, were given the Normal and Super models, respectively. The mild version produced 60 hp at 4500 rpm on a 7.5:1 compression ratio, while the Super did 15 hp better at 5000 on 8.5:1—a reflection of the improvement in fuel octane rating. The smaller-displacement engines would continue on until September 1957 and until then, both 1300 and 1600 Supers used the roller-bearing crank and larger 40 PICB carbs on new cast manifolds, though some of the smaller engines were built with 32 PBIC units. The transmission mounts were doubled up on a new nosepiece, and a

The Porsche-Schlepper Type 111 was built by Allgaier from the late 1940s until 1955, when a new alliance was set up between Porsche and the Mannesman group to build a new tractor plant. Porsche

82

revised release bearing made the driveline smoother and stronger

On December 1, 1955, the US Army officially returned the original Porsche Zuffenhausen buildings to the company. The day was, coincidentally, the twenty-fifth anniversary of the founding of the Porsche Design Bureau. Most of the administrative staff moved there including Hans Kern and the financial group, purchasing agent Karl Kirn and the sales head, Walter Schmidt. Hans Klauser, Porsche's point man in the return to Stuttgart, was now in charge of sales-related technical affairs.

Klaus Von Rücker, a former Studebaker executive, joined the firm at this time, stepping in to carry on the work of Albert Prinzing, who had left to manage a new tractor firm, *Porsche-Diesel-Moterenbau GmbH*. Allgaier had built 25,000 Porsche-designed tractors since 1947, but Prinzing and Porsche saw greater opportunities with a larger company. The Mannesmann group funded a new factory in Friederichshafen that

The Porsche Type 597 Jagdwagen project was undertaken without any government contract but after another military vehicle was chosen for army use, the Hunter was offered to the public. Seventy-one were built in two versions through 1958. It used a single-carb 1488cc *and later 1582 cc Porsche engine with a gearbox that resembled the Cisitalia's. Four-wheel drive could be engaged, and the unit was floatable though not powered in the water. Porsche*

built tractors in large quantities until the mid 1960s with royalties going to Porsche.

Design work was continuing for VW and other clients at the same time. Porsche even got involved in military vehicles again with the design of Type 597, a four-wheel-drive Kübelwagen-type vehicle. The project was begun in late 1953 with the assumption that it could be easily sold to the German army, now rearming in the face of the cold war. In testing, the *Jagdwagen* proved worthy, but a competitor's vehicle was chosen in a political maneuver that left Ferry Porsche with a determination to, in his words, "never again lift a finger in this section unless there was a firm order on the table." The Hunter, as the car was known, was offered to the public in 1955, but by 1958 only seventy-one were built.

In the mid 1950s, Porsche began to get orders from people who did not fit the normal profile of a sports car enthusiast. Highway policemen in Germany and other European countries found that white 356A cabriolets suited their needs admirably. Giving up their Volkswagens and Mercedes 220 sedans, the North Rhine Westphalia autobahn police were among many constabularies who complemented their new mounts with white overcoats and helmets, not to mention the

lights, horns and two-way radio. The high-profile image of these uniformed peace officers in open white Porsches became a tradition that carries on to this day.

Americans got bumper overriders on their Porsches in 1956, reflecting the difficulties owners faced in navigating the sea of heavy chrome that their highways were becoming. The year 1957 brought more changes, but for the most part they were subtle or invisible. Normal engines got an aluminum cam gear. Carburetors were warmed by air from the heat exchangers through tubes in the rear of the engine apron. Teardrop-shaped taillights replaced the twin circles, and the rear license and back-up light became a shine-up rather than shine-down affair. Some trim items were changed in what was becoming a Porsche tradition: phasing in new parts only when existing stocks were depleted, rather than at the end of a model year. Enthusiasts in later years would puzzle over anomalies such as a V-front sunroof (matching the early bent windshields) in a 356A Carrera with curved glass.

A new transmission called Type 644 was phased in slowly during the year. Its main section was cast and machined in a single piece rather than bolted together with a vertical split as before. Gear clusters were mounted to an aluminum inter-

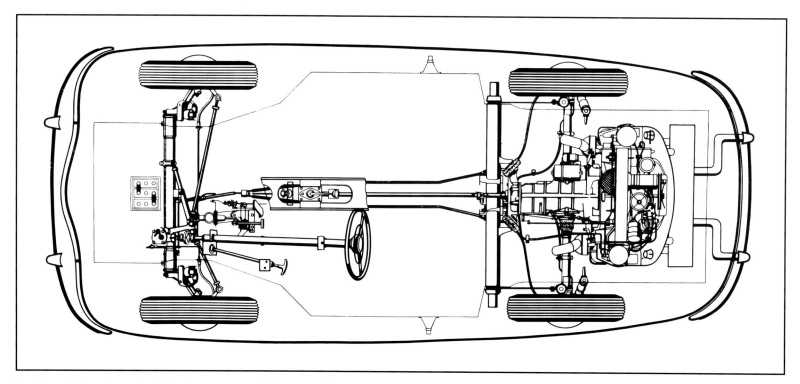

The T-2 body and mechanical changes were all but invisible, except for the routing of exhaust pipes through the bumperettes.

Type 356-001, the first car to bear the Porsche name, consisted of a simple tube frame and aluminum body. It was sold to a Swiss enthusiast and in the mid 1950s bought back by the factory. Now restored to near-original condition, it maintains a place of honor in the Porsche museum. Porsche

The original 356 shape has been described as religiously functional and Erwin Komenda surely worshiped at the altar of efficiency.

Smooth and clean, the aluminum Gmünd cars have a look that is quite distinct from the coupes that followed.

The Gmünd coupe sported a single tiny exhaust pipe from its 40 hp engine, but that was almost twice the power of the Volkswagen from which it derived.

Ferdinand is an early Zuffenhausen coupe, originally presented to Professor Ferdinand Porsche on the occasion of his seventy-fifth birthday. After his death, it went to the test department where it became the first 1500, the first Carrera and the first Porsche to try many other innovations. Porsche

Chassis 5014 from 1950 was one of the first Reutter-built cabriolets. Though not large, the Porsche cabriolet was a plush and pleasant touring car, this one even sporting whitewall tires. Its dashboard shows an optional tachometer and other custom touches that were popular in the early 1950s. Horn buttons were a common means of showing individuality, as if owning a Porsche in 1950 was not rare enough.

A number of Gmünd coupes were pressed into racing service for two main reasons: they were light and they were expendable. Customers preferred the improved Stuttgart cars, so a few left-over models became the first Porsches to win real racing laurels. This car, with a lowered roof and other track adaptations, proudly wears its competition record on the door. Porsche

Most racers don't consider a hacksaw to be a performance-improvement tool, but Johnny von Neumann thought that the aluminum coupe he was unsuccessfully racing would go faster without the weight of the roof. Sans top and Le Mans-type skirts, the car was a winner at the Torrey Pines, California, sports car race in July 1951 and it continued racing for a few more years in other hands. Chuck Forge has owned the car since 1957 and restored it to again look like von Neumann's winning mount from 1952. Hal Thoms

Predecessor to the America Roadster and spiritual forebear to the Speedster, Heinrich Sauter's custom-built racer was restored to its original condition in the mid 1980s by Ray Knight. Seen here in its natural element, the Jaguar-like rear fenders were out of character for an Erwin Komenda design, but reflected contemporary style and probably the influence of Max Hoffman. Hal Thoms

The 1954 Cabriolets were refined from the earliest cars, but most of the changes were under the skin.

The A Series carried the new 1600 engine for 1956, with the oil filter canister above, added the year before, and the carb linkage below, which would be changed soon.

The rear seat back in this 1956 A coupe is a single unit that hinges to provide luggage room, since the trunk is mostly tank and tire.

In the Speedster, if you wanted options, you put them in yourself. A radio could be bolted under the dash and there was plenty of floor space for an ashtray. This early Speedster had a small central gauge, while later cars had the tach moved to the middle with a larger combination dial on the right. Mostly original, this car shows the effect of sun and elements over the years.

The Speedster got the nickname "Bathtub" for obvious reasons.

Porsche's low-price model was the first to wear rocker panel deco strips, which became standard on other cars, and the bright beltline spear that was seen on many later models. Like the America Roadster before it and the Convertible D and B Roadster that came later, it was distinguished from the cabriolet by a removable windshield. This beautifully restored Speedster benefits from the addition of rally lights, C disc brakes, 911 alloy wheels and a tweaked engine— tasteful modifications that enhance the car's sporting character.

The Speedster, Convertible D (shown here) and Roadster were meant as two-place automobiles with luggage space behind the seats. Cushions were available for what Porsche called "emergency" seating.

The Roadster, built by both Drauz and later, D'Ieteren, was much like the Speedster at first glance. Plush seats, roll-up windows and nicely finished door panels were the main interior differences. The Nardi wood steering wheel was an option and a popular aftermarket item for a number of years.

Headlight stoneguards and auxiliary lighting were not a bad idea on a high-speed touring car. The side spear of polished aluminum, first seen on the Speedster, became a popular option on other cars in the line.

The GT bodies had aluminum doors and lids, but not necessarily four-cam motors. In a late 1950s press release, Porsche had mentioned color-coding Super and Normal engines with red and blue fan housings, but only grey and black are normally seen. Velocity stacks help smooth the flow of air at higher rpm, but their length must be tuned to the specific engine. Seen here is the late-style carb linkage that pivots from a shaft mounted in front of the fan. A fire suppression system can be seen pointed at the carbs. Without having a choke, Porsche carbs were known to backfire on startup occasionally, and fires were not uncommon.

The Speedster is dead, long live the Speedster. It was the same body and the same spirit, but the raw-boned character was gone. The Convertible D had plush seats, finished door panels and an all-weather top, with a higher windshield that changed the look of the car dramatically.

The 1961 Roadster carried on in the Speedster tradition, incorporating the new T-5 B body.

Lightweight GT bodies made extensive use of aluminum and when combined with the Super 90 engine were respectable performers on the street or the track.

A 1958 Carrera Speedster GT with cold air boxes that envelop the air cleaners. The Sebring exhaust gave minimal interference to exiting gases. Aluminum bumpers, trim strips and wheel rims were part of the weight-conscious GT program as well. Aluminum hubcaps were supplied with GTs, but most owners thought, "Why bother?" The license plate on this car distills into two words the proper way to drive a Carrera.

The A Series ended with the 1959 models. Some of the changes during the A years were a license light swap—from above to below—and teardrop taillights. Some owners opted for the Speedster seats, and in later years a common modification was the installation of wider wheels. Rear bumperettes would discolor easily from the exhaust pipes routed through them, so the easy solution was to remove them. William Miller

These two coupes are actually three generations apart. The early A on the left still has twin round taillights, later changed to teardrops with the T-2 body in 1957. The Super 90 on the right is a second-generation B with T-6 body, including twin grilles and larger rear window. The deck shape had changed subtly but surely, and the bumper height difference is also evident.

Lovely but unloved, the Karmann Hardtop Coupe had a short life between 1961 and 1962. This T-6 bodied example has the normal 60 hp engine, identified by its horsepower rating on the rear.

Between the end of the roadster line and the introduction of the T-6 body there was a short overlap of models that produced the "Twin-Grille Roadster." Shown here after a fresh paint job, the squared-off hood shape, gas filler opening and gas tank are clearly seen. First versions of the new tank used a bottom-mounted gauge sender which was soon changed to the top-mount version on this car. A formed-plastic cover gave the trunk a finished look. Speedster seats and wood steering wheels were often ordered or retrofitted in all kinds of Porsches. Crested hubcaps were an option at first, and later standard. Rivertown Carrozzeria

This true four-seater Porsche, built by Beutler in Thun, Switzerland, was based on the 356B. Beutler's association with Porsche dated to the Gmünd days when they built some of the first cabriolets, and since 1957, they had produced four-passenger coupes and open cars on VW pans, using Porsche mechanicals.

The C model was the last of the line, and after sixteen years, the most comfortable and well-mannered. Though trunk space and rear seat space were both enlarged a bit, luggage racks continued to be a popular option. Flat hubcaps were a giveaway to the Dunlop disc brakes behind and the round Durant side mirror was new. Exhaust extensions helped prevent chrome discoloration on the bumper uprights.

The C cabriolet was the most civilized convertible Porsche ever built, the last in a long line of open cars that began in Gmünd. With the end of the 356 line, Porsche customers had to wait almost two decades for another true convertible. The Targa bar on the 901 series was touted as a safety item and though it undoubtedly did give better rollover protection, many customers missed the traditional topless version.

The 2.0 liter Type 587 four-cam engine was wider than the earlier Carrera powerplants, and made servicing even more of a headache. The license plate on this Carrera 2 cabriolet sums up the plight of a modern-day owner in need of parts. "New old stock" is the equivalent of buying an antique part still new in the box. "No longer available" is just what it says.

A Carrera engine on the stand at Jim Wellington's shop. Earlier versions had distributors connected to the intake cam ends. The four plugs on each bank were not easily accessible with the engine installed in a 356.

The 904 had few ties with the 356, other than the four-cam engine. Chronologically, it shared production with the 356C, but its significance lies in its creation as a tour de force by yet another Ferdinand

Porsche, the grandson of the old Professor. The 904 is also a link in the chain of Le Mans-style endurance racers that extends from the aluminum Gmünd coupes to the 956 and 962, seen in the background.

The Porsche Club of America staged a Tribute to Le Mans at its 1990 Parade in Monterey. Here at Laguna Seca the front row is made up of 550s and 718s with a wide variety of machinery behind.

Variations on a theme, or, a nose by any other name. From the first 550s with near-vertical headlights, the front of the Spyders evolved into a lower and more streamlined affair with faired-in or covered-over headlights. Round extensions on the lower lip of some cars could carry lights or horns, useful when the race course went along public roads in rural areas.

The last of the RS series saw private duty on the racetracks for years after the factory had gone to larger and more sophisticated engines. This nicely restored example sports the FIA-required tall windshield and a comprehensive history on its side.

The 550 Spyders are distinguishable from the 718 by the nose shape, even under a cover. Also waiting in the Paddock are a GT coupe and an Abarth Carrera. Hal Thoms

Few 356 bodies are discarded these days. Even basket cases like this ex-coupe are being salvaged. Right-hand drive Speedsters did not exist—until now, but this "coupster" will carry a plaque stating its origin.

This kind of traffic jam could only occur during a 356 Registry meet.

mediate plate that fit between the main housing and the nose-piece, and the assembly was inserted through one open end of the casting, giving rise to the name "tunnel case." It was a stronger unit all around and offered easier servicing than the 519 and as with the earlier synchro box, offered a choice of ratios in each gear.

T-2 Body

At the fall 1957 Frankfurt Auto Show, Technische Program 2 (T-2) cars were unveiled. Most of the news was in the engine department—the 1300 was history, as was the Hirth crankshaft. Normal engines got cast-iron cylinders for a cost savings and quieter operation. Oil temperature senders were moved out behind the new, more effective oil coolers and a thermostatic valve now diverted the flow of oil when the engine was cold. Zenith carbs with replaceable venturis were put to use on both Normal (24 mm) and Super (32 mm) engines and were mounted on dual-tube manifolds. Carb linkage was changed to lever arms working from a shaft in front of the fan shroud for more consistent control.

A new diaphragm pressure plate replaced the spring-type unit used previously, and the shifter was moved back while the heater knob moved toward the front of the car. Along with a larger 425 mm steering wheel, a new stud-and-worm steering box built by ZF was installed, but ironically, it was not a Porsche design. It was, however, slightly more direct and

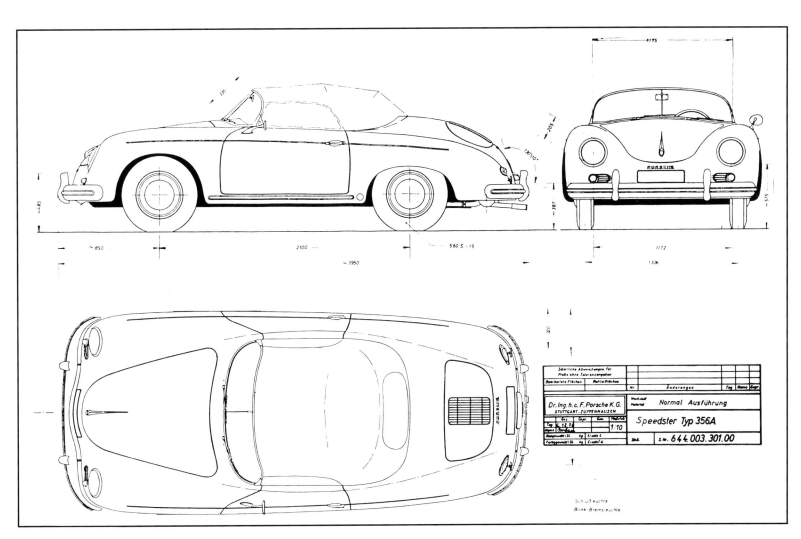

Introduced at the end of 1954, the Speedster received numerous updates along with the rest of the line. Although outwardly similar, the first and last of the Speedsters had different taillights, tops, instruments and a host of mechanical changes.

easier with fewer turns lock-to-lock. Astute observers would notice the doors had repositioned striker plates and a new outside handle shape. Another feature of these 1958 models was the reintroduction of vent windows on the cabriolet, gone since Gmünd days and the lack of which was one of few consistent criticisms leveled against the car. In a move that smacked of Detroit glitz, the exhaust pipes were routed through the lower part of the bumperettes, gaining some ground clearance at the back, and new hubcaps with a raised Porsche crest were available and standard on the Super. The cab's rear cowl was modified to accept a removable hardtop—now one could have the best of both worlds.

A transmission change was made in 1958, incorporating advancements in the ring synchronizer design by Leopold Schmid. By dividing the servo functions among additional parts, the new transmission was cheaper to build, easier to use in downshifts and gave heavy-handed drivers a better chance to shift smoothly. Installed in the same case as the 644 transmission, it was given the type number 716 and beginning in December 1958, was used in the coupes and cabriolets. Standard gearing was BBBC with a 4.43:1 final-drive ratio. Some testers bemoaned the changes, as voiced in a 1960 issue of *Sports Car Illustrated* magazine: "The increased blocking of the revised synchro has some less than happy side effects. On shifts from third to second, for instance, if you don't double-clutch, that 'slicing through butter' feel just isn't there any-more.... All the changes will be justified, however, if the new gearbox is less delicate and offers the owner fewer mainte-nance headaches."

Speedster Type 540

The Yanks were buying sports cars like crazy in the mid 1950s and a good many of these were MG and Triumph con-vertibles that were considerably less expensive than the Stutt-gart models. Max Hoffman, determined to keep his Porsche franchise miles ahead in sales, had been importing the Amer-ica Normal coupes and cabriolets. For 1955, a stripper model was continued but the entire line was renamed Continental,

The rocker panel deco and polished aluminum side spear were added to the Speedster after the first cars were built in fall 1954. These distinctive trim items soon became a part of the entire line.

Pike's Peak, July 1961

Carrying on in the tradition of Otto Mathé and a host of European hill climbers, Jack Gwynn takes on Pike's Peak. Here was one race where the car was completely in its element. Dave Friedman

Pomona, California, August 1962

Speedsters were put to use on racetracks immediately, and stayed there for years. This early "bathtub" is still going strong at a Pomona, California, SCCA race in 1962. A propped-open engine lid helped cool the engine. Dave Friedman

this time with the name in script on the fender. Americans were used to cars with fancy designations, no matter how ridiculous they sounded, and Hoffman saw to it that his Porsches carried more than cold Teutonic numbers. But Ford was not long in challenging the use of a name they owned for their Lincolns, since they were poised to introduce a new Continental and took a dim view of anyone else using the name. Porsche beat a hasty retreat, but in the last months of 1955 the America/Continental concept was carried on with the name European. By the beginning of 1956, the script and the name were gone and the coupes and cabriolets went back to number designations. Porsche stated that the reason for the names was "to adopt to U.S. habit marking vehicles with designations." True enough, Hoffman knew that Americans related better to names than numbers. And starting in 1954 he was selling a new Porsche with a catchy name, an attractive price and a personality that would make it one of the best-known cars of all time—the Speedster.

The challenge from other makes brought Hoffman to Albert Prinzing and Ferry Porsche with a request: build a simple, open roadster that he could sell for under $3,000. The light and lively aluminum America Roadsters had been a sensation, but they were much too expensive to make a broad impact on the market. With a fresh sheet of paper, the new design became a combination of cabriolet and America Roadster and was even given the same type number as that aluminum racetrack hero: 540.

The Speedster carried distinctive features both on the outside and in the cockpit. The cowl at the rear was considerably different from its cabriolet mates, being longer and with little pretense of a back seat attempted, though a seat cushion and back were optional. The rocker panels wore aluminum and rubber deco strips and a brightmetal spear ran above the beltline through the door handles. First seen on the Speedster, these trim items would become a regular part of the line. The top was simple and easy to fold, but gave little real protection from the elements. Fastened to the low windshield frame, it gave less a feeling of security than claustrophobia and at speed, the removable side curtains flapped as energetically as the top. As a finishing touch, the little upside-down-bathtub-shaped car wore its name on each front fender.

Interior appointments were spare but efficient. The gauges were clustered under a curved and padded hood with the necessary knobs nearby. The simplest of door panels complemented the nearest thing to racing seats that most customers had yet seen. Hinged at the lower front, the whole seat shell lifted forward to give access to the small area behind. It was a basic, no-frills machine—if you wanted a radio, you would have to find a place to install it—but like every other Porsche, it was a quality piece. Reutter's bodywork was impeccable, a choice of engines was available and best of all, it was priced at $2,995 in New York. Whether any Speedsters were ever sold for that price is a matter of conjecture, since standard equipment did not include two items: a heater and a tachometer. The

Mankato, Minnesota, August 1961
Just before the start of a race at Mankato, Tom Countryman's Speedster joins a host of other Porsches, MGAs and at the rear, "Bugeye"

Sprites. The small-displacement classes were hotly contested and the Speedster, here shown with a custom tonneau cover, was the favored model for short-track competition. Tom Countryman

Riverside, March 1962

In a well-choreographed move, three Speedsters take a turn at Riverside. From left, Charlie Gates, Dave Jordan and Allen Johnson demonstrate that individual preferences in suspension setting and driving techniques can each be effective in their own way. Note the excessive rear camber on car number 110. Dave Friedman

heater may not have been a necessity, but the tachometer was. At almost 200 lb. lighter than the other models, it was a natural for the racetrack, and shorter third and fourth gears gave it a decidedly sporting character.

Introduced in September 1954, the new model found its way to the production-car racing circuits in a hurry. Johnny von Neumann won a Torrey Pines, California, race just after Thanksgiving, the first of a string of Speedster victories that extends to the present day. As West Coast distributor, his dealership on Ventura Boulevard in North Hollywood became a primary source for West Coast racers who couldn't afford a Spyder but wanted a light and competitive car. It was an

Pomona, California, July 1962
When is a Speedster not a Speedster? When it's a stripped-for-racing Convertible D, here being demonstrated by Roger Barscher at Po- mona in 1962. Take away the higher windshield and top, the nice interior and you are almost back to the old bare-bones bathtub. Dave Friedman

entry-level Porsche before the term existed and Californians took to the car immediately. The impractical nature of such a beast was a foregone conclusion in most climes, but here was a

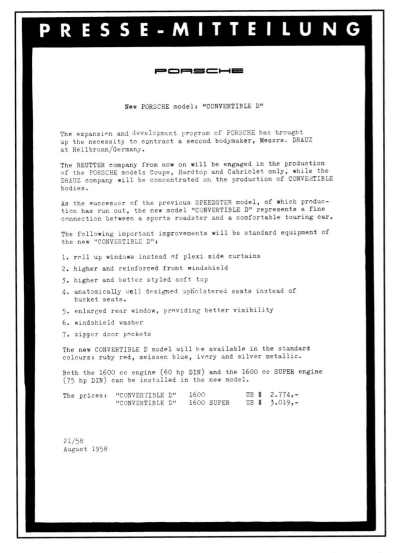

At Porsche there were few tears shed over the demise of the Speedster. This enthusiastic press release simply states that "production has run out" and touts the amenities of the new model. What is not mentioned is the extra hundred pounds and the fact that delivered prices were considerably higher than those shown here. But the third paragraph is right on the mark in describing the intended use of the new car—a combination of sports and touring. Road & Track

car that seemed to be made just for the Golden State. No one cared if the top leaked. As a matter of fact, the cars often leaked more at the base of the removable windshield than at the top, but at least that solid Reutter floor pan didn't let any water in. Of course, it didn't let any water out either, and the nickname "Bathtub" came from more than just the car's shape.

The first Speedsters could be equipped with 1500 Normal or Super engines and later, shared most of the chassis and powerplant upgrades given the rest of the line. The light but cramped removable top assembly was given a bit more height in the second and third bows and a larger rear window sometime in 1957. California boat builder Glaspar offered a $285 fiberglass hardtop for the car in 1955 and two years later the factory adopted a similar item, selling it through dealers. For everyday motoring, at least two other companies made hardtops of varying designs but for the purists, the Speedster was at its best top down, tail out, twisting through the turns.

For Porsche, this simple machine expanded both the price range and the model range but the truth is, it was never really taken to heart by Zuffenhausen. Ferry Porsche felt that stripping a car was not the way to increase sales, and the Speedster, designed from the start as a no-frills car, was not as well received by European enthusiasts who after years of postwar privation had come to appreciate the marque for its quality and amenities.

Convertible D

At the end of August 1958, a successor to the Speedster was announced: the Convertible D. In many ways familiar, the new version of Porsche's simple roadster featured a higher windshield with a commensurately higher canvas top and larger rear window. Roll-up door windows, comfortable cabriolet-style seats and more elaborate door trim reflected in the $3,695 price tag, only slightly less than the coupe. Its 1,900 lb. weight was almost up to the coupe, but with the same BBAB gearing as the Speedster, it retained some of the old zip. The D in the name stood for Drauz, the Karosserie in nearby Heilbronn that built the bodies for Porsche. Welcomed by many but frowned upon by those who missed its Spartan forerunner, the D was the last permutation in the 356A series. More than 1,300 were built in the 1958 and 1959 model years, about twenty percent of the production total, but after less than two years it was gone. In September there was a new roadster, a new engine and a completely new look for the entire Porsche line-up.

Riverside, March 1962
The B coupes were heavier, but still competitive. Here at Riverside,

California, a Super 90 driven by Miles Gopton maintains the Stuttgart tradition of sideways cornering. Dave Friedman

Chapter 9

The 356 B and C Series

Polishing the Jewel

Gradual and studied changes took place in the 356 model range during its first decade. Though each new item was carefully examined and exhaustively tested before inclusion in the car, many of the advancements were all but invisible. The American practice of using flashy body styling changes to make a technically "old" car seem "new" was shunned by Porsche. Indeed, just the opposite was true. But after the September 1959 Frankfurt Auto Show, the company

Porsche, Zuffenhausen, 1961
With the 356B, Porsche achieved the milestone of 50,000 cars—a hundred times the number originally planned, and more than 26,000 more to come. Road & Track

was accused of "going Detroit" with the introduction of a completely revised car, the 356B.

The obvious American influence on this T-5 body began with the bumpers, which were now nearly 4 in. higher in the front and rear. They looked bulky, but with sheet-metal construction they had little in common with the massive American bumper, other than height. Large vertical bumperettes, overrriders and underriders, seemed to say, "don't mess with me!" The headlights were raised to the more angular peak of the fender and underneath, highly stylized louvered openings appeared below as well as above the bumper. The turn signals were now mounted on extended chrome bases and the hood handle was larger. While the hood shape remained the same as the A series, the new car's hood had a flatter contour. From the cowl back, the body exterior remained similar to the previous model, though the rear bumper mounting points at the side of the body were indented slightly. The chrome assembly formerly used for license and back-up lighting disappeared; two lights mounted on the bumper top surface and a small enclosed unit under the bumper did these duties. Reflectors, which had been used ever since 1952, were now typically placed either under the bumper on European cars or above the taillight on American cars.

Inside, the three-spoke steering wheel was dished somewhat and finished in black plastic to match the rest of the knobs, including the gearshift on its new chrome-plated stalk. A central horn button was standard, with a horn ring available optionally. Porsche had developed a hydraulically damped telescopic safety steering column, but its very design would not permit its use in the 356. Turn signal switches now doubled as headlight dimmers, and vent windows returned to all models but the Roadster. In the back seat, any masochist desiring to sit there could now have an easier time of it. The area on either side of the transmission hump was lowered by 2 in. and a split seatback was now standardized. New heater slides over the tube opening on the inside of the doorsill and rear window defogger vents were other noticeable changes, but some of the most important ones were not readily seen.

Behind the wheels and crested hubcaps were new brakes based on a stronger aluminum drum with ferrous inserts bonded to the aluminum by the Alfin process. Better heat dissipation was achieved with seventy-two lateral fins on the

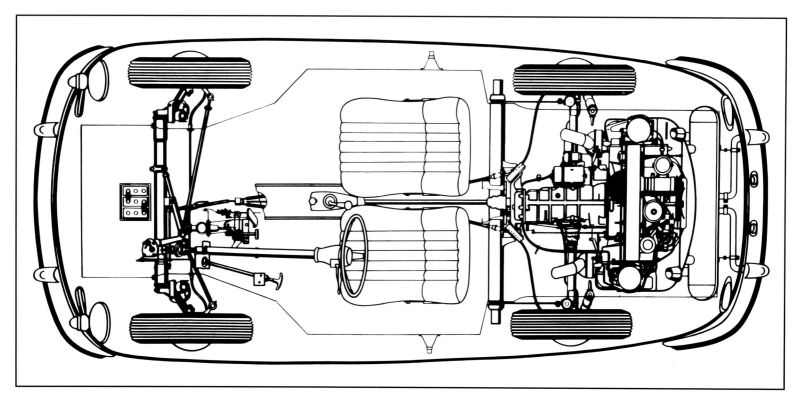

In plain view, the rounded nose and larger bumpers of the 356B are evident. Porsche

outer edge, a design proven on early Spyders. New linings and better water sealing complemented the drum improvement and at the front, stronger spindles with roller bearings kept it all in place. Porsche had been experimenting with disc brakes but they were still a few years off for the production cars. In the meantime, the new drums were adequate under most conditions.

The 716 gearbox was given a mild nose job and renamed the 741. A repositioned single rubber mount at the front permitted the lowering of the rear seat, but this arrangement allowed the transmission to roll about its axis, affecting rear wheel geometry. After 3,000 units were built the engineers went back to a double-mount as in the earlier 644, renaming it Type 741, version II. Also incorporated was a sleeve around the output shaft over which the throwout bearing could travel without rocking on its pivots—a definite help to adjustment.

Super 90 Type 616/7

The Type 616/1 and 616/2 engines were joined by another in March of 1960. Introduced with the T-5 body in September, it took some months before production of the new 616/7 motor got under way. Called the Super 90 in honor of its power output, its head featured larger ports and 40 mm intake valves, up 2 mm from the Super. Stronger rocker arms rode on a new aluminum carrier with light pushrods, and stronger single valve springs evolved from those used the previous two years. Cast-aluminum manifolds held 40 PII-4 Solex carbs and mesh air cleaners. At the heart of the engine was a crank with larger main bearing journals and nitride-hardened surfaces to work with the new lead-bronze bearings. Stronger rods connected to 9.0:1 compression pistons with three compression rings. Aluminum cylinder inner surfaces were coated with molybdenum steel in a process called Ferral. The flywheel was lightened by almost 5 lb., allowing quicker acceleration and with the stronger and lighter valve components, it could rev safely to 6000 rpm. The Super 90 generator was a 200 watt unit, 40 more than its lesser brethren.

Porsche had been thinking of the hotshoes who couldn't afford a Carrera when designing the Super 90. On the matter of losing lubrication in tight corners, racers of earlier cars had a number of ways to deal with it. Some mounted a big taillight to the steering column to supplement the oil pressure light on the dash. When the light flashed on, you knew it was time to back off. A preventative approach was to install a windage tray, basically a horizontal shelf that kept the bulk of the oil in the bottom of the crankcase. Porsche foresaw the new Super 90 getting some track use, as witnessed in their own oil scavenging arrangement. A new assembly was built around the oil pickup tube in the crankcase using sliding valves. In hard

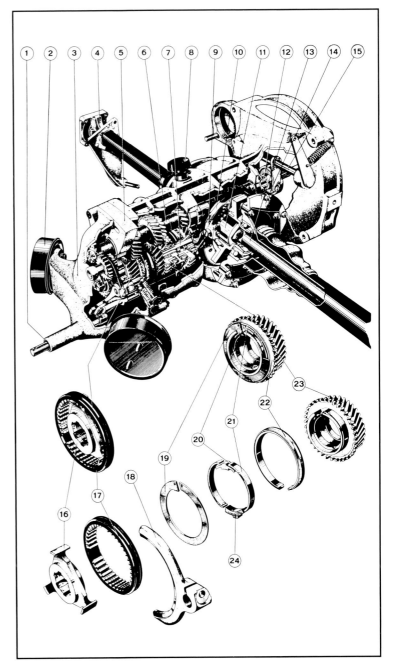

The Type 741 transmission version II reverted to double front mounts. This second-generation synchromesh unit featured the newer style split-ring (22) and accompanying bands (21) first used in 1958 in the tunnel-case transmission housing from 1957. A further improvement was the twelve-bolt differential housing used in the 356C models. Standard with the 1600 coupe was a BBBC gear set, and the Roadster, Super and S-90 engines came with a D fourth gear. Porsche

Porsche, Zuffenhausen, 1962
Production of the 356B in T-6 form. This photo shows that the assembly line has doubled in size from the mid 1950s. The high-quality, handbuilt aspect of construction was maintained through the life of the 356 and beyond. Porsche

cornering when centrifugal force would move the oil to one side of the case, the valve would slide to open on that same side, so the pickup point was always in the oil. Another part of the engine's life insurance policy was a bypass valve that came into play upon start-up, sending oil directly to the bearings before routing any to the cooler. It is particularly ironic that after all the consideration given to lubricating this engine, there were numerous initial crankshaft failures, remedied by lengthening the oil pump gears for more volume.

A last S-90 improvement gave the cooling fan smoother airflow by deleting the screen and adding a rounded flange to its opening. The cylinder shrouds below gave the air a more direct downward flow, adding up to a nearly ten percent increase in cooling efficiency. Many of these improvements were incorporated into the 1600 and 1600 S engines during the next two years, along with a few additional modifications to the suspension.

Dunlop radial tires were available after five years of testing on Spyders and road cars. Michelin and Continental also did cooperative testing with the Zuffenhausen engineers, but the association with Dunlop was the most productive and the end result was the 165x15 CB59 tire, standard on the Super 90

and Carrera. Working in tandem with the new tires were Dutch Koni shocks and a new innovation, a camber compensating spring at the rear. This device consisted of a single leaf spring connected at its ends to each swing axle just inside the from hub, with the transmission resting on its center where a simple pin held the spring. Since the spring now supported some of the rear weight, the torsion bars were narrowed from 24 to 23 mm, giving the rear less roll stiffness and allowing the front tires to do more to support the car in a turn.

In racing circles, the pushrod-engined cars did not make headlines anymore—that distinction was now held by the Spyders and Carreras—but at the Nüburgring in June 1959, Edgar Barth took a pre-production Super 90 around the course in 11.08 seconds, about as fast as most four-cams could do it. In the 1,000 km race later that week, the lightweight car was thirteenth overall and only fractionally slower than the fastest Carrera. This was the public debut of the new engine with the improved brakes and compensating spring that would accompany it in production nine months later.

Road testers of the B Super 90 were unstinting in their praise for the improved handling, powerful engine and interior appointments. The standard 1600 was described in *Sports Car Illustrated* as having a "'squirrelly' feel that's deceptive... until you're used to the car." The article continued, "but it's on the bumpy back roads that this car really performs wonders. You find yourself searching for serpentine, climbing, diving and winding byways just to exploit the astonishing agility of this car. The surface doesn't matter; the bumpier it is, the more the Porsche likes it." Particularly appreciative were owners who had to deal with rough roads on a regular basis. A 1961 road test in *Sports Car World* chronicled an Australian outing, much of it spent on rural backroads with four people aboard in a 1600 Super equipped with front bench seat and whitewall tires!

The magazines liked them, the customers liked them and in 1961 there were more Porsches than ever to like. The Roadster, in its second year, inherited the role of the Speedster and Convertible D, but was not really a simple open car anymore. True, its unpadded top was not as sophisticated as the cabriolet's, but the rest of the car was almost as nicely appointed as any other Porsche and it even weighed more than the standard coupe. The Roadster was built in its final year by both Drauz and a Belgian coachmaker, D'leteren Frères, who constructed bodies and assembled entire cars. The last of these appeared in late 1961 with T-6 body updates as 1962 models. In Zuffenhausen, Reutter was building coupe bodies in standard and lightweight form for the GT cars, along with cabriolets that could also be had with the steel hardtop. Some customers opted to buy the car with only one top, so certain open cars actually spent their lives as hardtops. Porsche must have thought that particular shape was pleasing enough to produce as a fixed-roof version, so they did.

Joining the list of body suppliers in 1961 was Karmann Karosserie in Osnabrück, Germany. Karmann had a long history of auto body building dating from 1908, and carriages before that. Fords, DKWs, VW cabriolets and Ghias rolled off the lines there in the 1950s and were joined by a new Porsche bodystyle in early 1961. The notchback, as it became known, was a cross between the cabriolet hardtop and the coupe, and not surprisingly, was called the hardtop coupe. What was achieved with the notchback was slightly better visibility and not much else—certainly not increased sales, since the model never become popular. But increased sales was Porsche's aim in spreading the assembly work around, although the logistics of using four separate companies to do it were becoming a problem. By the next year only two body suppliers would remain: Reutter producing cabriolets and coupes, and Karmann making the notchback and their own standard version of the coupe. The B chassis was also the basis for a true four-seat automobile that was made in Thun, Switzerland, by Beutler.

The steady increase in production numbers necessitated more room for assembly and related operations. In September 1959, Werk III was completed and some of the sales, parts and delivery operations moved there from Werk II where the

The Karmann Hardtop Coupe was a separate body style, but not particularly popular.

assembly area then expanded. A few months later, finance chief Hans Kern and Ghislaine Kaes began a search to find even more space, this time for a test and development center. A ninety-three-acre parcel was found near Weissach, just a few miles east of Stuttgart, that suited the needs outlined by Ferry Porsche with one exception: it was considerably more land than he felt the company could afford. But soon enough, Kern's foresight was acknowledged and ground was broken for a skidpad in October 1961.

In the fall of 1961, a body makeover took place and the 356 models, all fourteen combinations of engine and bodystyles, were given the designation T-6, the last variation in the shape of the original Porsche. A larger rear window with twin engine grilles at the rear and a more squared-off front trunk were the obvious clues to the new body. On the coupe and cabriolet's front cowl was a grille to take in fresh air, an improvement

that had been a long-time coming. Cabriolet owners could now enjoy a zip-open rear window, and vent (with optional fan) controls were at the center of the dash, above the clock—another item that should have been standard years before. Conversely, Porsche anticipated public demand with the inclusion of locking seatbacks, a break-away mirror and a gearshift lock on its base.

With a new trunk arrangement, an old problem was solved, at least for owners of left-hand-drive cars. The need to keep a close watch on gas attendants had always been an integral part of Porsche ownership. Getting under the hood was required for a fill-up, and closing it was a matter of lifting slightly to release a catch, then gently lowering and if necessary, applying gentle pressure at the chrome handle. Many well-meaning gas jockeys would pull straight down on the hood until it bent, only then realizing that maybe they were

The new T-6 body was big news, judging by the number of times this photo appeared in period publications. The squared-off trunk lid and fuel filler are evident, as is the larger rear window on the new model. The woman is obviously wondering how to get back into her white B

coupe and is just about to notice that her side-view mirror has been stolen, perhaps by the same thoughtless driver who parked so close. Porsche

doing it wrong. The T-6 gas tank was redesigned to fit lower in the trunk and finally had an external filler—and not just a hole in the right fender, but a nicely contoured door with an inside spring release and rubberized "bib" that folded out to protect the paint. With this rearrangement of the trunk came a slight increase in luggage room, and a general tidying up of the space. A molded plastic cover hid the 13.2 gal. tank and under the tire, space was reserved for an optional gas heater, next to the battery in the nose. Fuses and washer bottle were conveniently placed against the firewall.

Along with the body changes, slight modifications were made to the Super 90 engine, which received a larger clutch, and to the 1600 Super, which got cast-iron cylinders from the Normal, the improved oil cooler and shrouding from the 90 and a new designation—616/12.

Polishing the Jewel: 356C

Waiting in the wings to take over the leading role in the Porsche line-up was a new creation, a modernized version of the car that by now had become known as the beloved bathtub. Styled by chief body designer Ferdinand Alexander Porsche, the 901 was undergoing road tests in the summer of 1963 when the final changes were made to the 356, meriting yet another designation, C. The only noticeable change in these 1964 models was that a flattened hubcap on a wheel with a bolt pattern became a tighter circle as Porsche abandoned for the first time the VW-style open-center wheel. But behind the wheel for the first time were new disk brakes.

Britain's *Car* magazine said of the drum brakes in late 1962, "they did fade quite noticeably on two distinct mountain passes. Never once did we feel we weren't going to stop, . . . it was just the brakes weren't 100 per cent with us for quite 100 per cent of the time. For that reason alone we recommend that Porsche get a move on with installing . . . disc brakes." The disk brakes that *Car* was referring to were Porsche's own—the annular design that was efficient and light, but expensive to build without the involvement of a company like Alfred Teves. Ate saw no future in the design for mass markets, however, and in fact they were trying to persuade Porsche to use the Dunlop design, which they could build for them at a reasonable cost.

With the end of its Formula racing involvement in 1962, Zuffenhausen gave up trying to further develop its own system and allowed Teves to incorporate some of their concepts into the Dunlop system for use in the last 356, and beyond. Single pistons operated on each side of the calipers and in the rear, a hat-shaped disk allowed two small shoes to operate as parking brakes, controlled by cable from under the dash as in the past. This innovation was one of the small, unseen but significant changes in the last of the original line.

Only two engines were offered in the final years of 1964 and 1965. Gone was the 60 Normal engine, and the 75 or 1600 Super became the 1600 C while the Super 90 was now called the SC. Both new engines were subtly changed under the direction of Hans Mezger, who recognized that the previous tradition of ever-enlarging the intake ports to get more horsepower had resulted in a breathing imbalance with the existing valve size, 40 and 31 mm. In an unprecedented step, he enlarged the exhaust valve to 34 mm and *reduced* the size of the intake by 2 mm to 38 mm for both engines. Ports were reshaped for more consistent cross section, and new contour chambers and piston shapes were used. The compression ratios were set at 8.5:1 for the C and 9.5:1 for the SC, which continued using the Super 90 cam while the C got a new higher-lift yet milder version. While the C carried on with cast-iron cylinders, the SC used Ferral cylinders at first, but in 1964 received a new Biral process cast-aluminum-over-iron sleeve unit.

Carburetion of the C engine was accomplished with Zenith NDIX 32s, and bigger 40 PII-4 carbs were used on the SC. The higher-output engine had a counterweighted crankshaft that gave it a power curve well up on the tach dial. A 95 hp at 5800 rpm rating seemed all but impossible from a pushrod engine not many years before, but with modern fuels and years of development, it could now be had for the price of a new SC: $4,745 for the coupe, $5,045 for the cabriolet. The C engine peaked at 5200 rpm, delivering 75 hp with a lower price of $4,295 and $4,595. For the big brother Carrera 2, you needed $7,595 and a long stretch of open highway, though the pushrod-engined cars were praised for their tractability in all kinds of traffic conditions.

Inside, the driver's seat was lowered to increase headroom, the heater knob became a lever and armrests joined the standard equipment list. With repositioned headlight and wiper knobs, these could be controlled without reaching through the steering wheel. The ashtray was now housed in a lower extension of the dash and on the right, the passenger grab handle was changed from chrome to black plastic. Suspension changes were minimal, but included larger torsion bars in front and smaller ones in the rear. A simple C or SC badge on the rear identified each model.

The Porsche company and the Porsche family were also making news. Ferdinand Alexander Porsche had joined his father's company in 1957, and in the mid 1960s was head of the newly established styling department where he was developing the shape of a new car to replace the 356. Another Ferdinand, Louise Piëch's son, joined the Porsche firm in 1963 and later became development chief. He went on to Audi where he became chairman of the board in the late 1980s. In 1964, Reutter was acquired by Porsche, except for the seat-making division, which was reestablished as Recaro, from Reutter Carrozzeria.

Journalists had been waxing eloquent for so many years that they hardly had anything to say about the new 356. Most road tests used the Carrera 2 as a subject, but those who did write about the bread-and-butter Porsches had a hard time finding fault. *Car and Driver*'s 1965 yearbook spent the first three paragraphs of an SC test complaining about the deletion of grease fittings on the door hinges and other weighty matters. In the same test, the magazine found, "The absence of the camber compensator has definitely impaired the Porsche's road-holding characteristics. . . . The 1600 Super we tested in the October, 1963, issue of *Car and Driver* had the device, and with it overcame almost all of our reservations about hurling rear-engined cars into strange corners." The rear spring was

The form-fitted gas tank in the T-6 gave a bit more trunk space and the outside gas filler was a welcome addition. The C series flat hubcaps indicated four-wheel disc brakes inside the wheels. Porsche tool kits always included items for roadside repairs well beyond changing tires, including a fan belt and spark plug wrench.

available for $48, while Koni shocks were a $41 option on the C, and standard on the two higher-powered cars, as were Michelin X or Continental radial tires.

Appearance and convenience options ranged from $78.50 chrome-plated wheels and Phoenix whitewalls for $29.40 (again, the American influence), all the way to a $312 electric sliding roof, the most expensive option on the list. Curiously, the Becker Grand Prix AM-FM radio, at $253, cost $31 more than an all-leather coupe interior. But offsetting the high cost of the car and its accessories was another dollar figure that gave particular satisfaction to both the builders and the buyers of the last 356 Porsches. $8.38 was the average cost of warranty service in the 1965 model year, and of course, after sixteen years of polishing, the German automotive jewel should indeed have been near perfection.

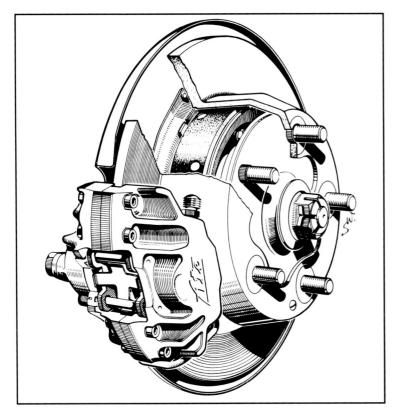

Uncharacteristically, Porsche waited years before adopting the discs made by Alfred Teves under license from Dunlop. Their own Type 695 annular ring disc was lighter but the cost of building them was prohibitive. Finally, with the last of the 356 series, the new ATE brakes and a heavier wheel to use with them were put into production. Shown here is the rear disc which includes a center drum parking brake.

End of an Era

The road that began at the former sawmill in Gmünd had led through racetracks and highways, mountain passes and back roads on every continent, and after sixteen years ended at the door of the Zuffenhausen factory in September 1965, as the last production 356, a white cabriolet, rolled to the end of the assembly line with flowers on its hood. It was the end of an era. In May 1966, Porsche built ten additional 356s for the Dutch police.

Under assembly in 1965 behind the last 356 in the factory were 911 and 912 models, thoroughly modern and already recognized as worthy successors to the car whose reputation had built the company. The 912 carried on the 356 bloodline by using the SC engine, in slightly detuned form, for another four years. The last of the 912s were built for the 1969 model year, incorporating an extension of the wheelbase and other improvements to the 901 series body. Series 616 industrial engines were still made into the 1970s, doing service as water pumps, electrical generators and other mundane tasks. But even as the factory phased out its last link with the original Porsche, private interest in the survival of the species was growing. The fact that they were no longer being built did not mean they were no longer being driven, or raced, or thoroughly enjoyed by enthusiasts. And the ranks of true believers have been swelling to include a new generation of drivers, new adherents to the *wishen* creed who are attracted by the same attributes that made the little car so beloved to so many.

Porsche, Zuffenhausen, September 1965
Goodbye, old friend. The last production 356 leaves the factory after some 76,300 were built. The initial run of 500 cars, deemed a risk in 1950, was extended beyond anyone's imagination in fifteen years of German production. Porsche

Pomona, California, August 1962
Vasek Polak was the ace tuner who not only fielded his own successful cars, but also showed the factory a few four-cam performance tips. Here Jack McAfee (88) and Ken Miles (50) demonstrate their Stuttgart hardware. Dave Friedman

Chapter 10

Rennsport Spyders

The Little Engine That Could

By the time the first aluminum coupe took the checkered flag at Le Mans in 1951, plans were already under way for a real competition machine, rather than an adapted road car. The Porsche philosophy of using light weight and balance to achieve performance was being carried out by other car makers, and often with greater success, especially for short events like the hillclimbs that were popular all over Germany. Walter Glöckler, a Volkswagen dealer from Frankfurt, along with Hermann Ramelow, an engineer who worked with him, built a VW-based special in 1950. Its ladder-type tubular frame held a Porsche Type 369, 1100 cc engine and VW running gear in the same configuration as the first 356 roadster. Its wheelbase was 2 in. shorter than the 356, at 80.7 in. Weighing just less than 1,000 lb., the mid-engine car won the 1.1 liter sports car championship that year, in addition to setting international class G records at Montlhéry in August.

Glöckler helped manage the Porsche effort at the same track in September 1951, and by this time he was closely aligned with the factory. His second Glöckler Special racer was again built by Weidenhausen of Frankfurt, but this time using a Porsche factory-supplied 1.5 liter Type 502 engine, the entire package weighing in at 990 lb. It carried a Porsche script on the nose and was referred to as the Glöckler-Porsche, reflecting a mutually beneficial program of promotion and technical assistance. This car joined the factory's two coupes in the record books that fall and in addition, won a hillclimb and a speedway event. Max Hoffman bought the car and shipped it to America where it was first raced, although unsuccessfully, in Florida in December. He did have some success in the spring of 1952, but sold the car to Ed Trego of Illinois soon afterward.

Driving that car was a challenge because of the leading-arm rear suspension, so the third Glöckler Special, finished early in 1952, used a shortened 356 chassis and indeed, had a marked resemblance to the production car in front. Walter's

cousin Helm drove the car to a 1500 cc championship that year, sometimes with a removable, aerodynamic roof in place. Max Hoffman brought this car to America too, where it did moderately well.

Other Glöckler Specials appeared the next year, one of which was on the Porsche stand in 1953 at the Geneva and Frankfurt Auto Shows.

Meanwhile in Zuffenhausen, Huschke von Hanstein, Karl Rabe and Ferry Porsche concluded that the progress being made by Italian OSCAs, East German EMWs and a host of other medium-displacement contenders had rendered the Gmünd coupes obsolete, and the Glöckler cars, attractive and competent, formed the basis on which the factory designed their new racers.

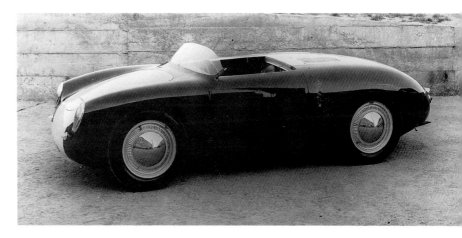

By 1953 the Glöckler Specials had evolved into beautiful, well-finished sports cars. This vehicle, built for Hans Stanek, used Porsche wheels and trim rings and a 1500 Super engine. It was shown on the Porsche stand at the Geneva and Frankfurt Auto Shows. Porsche

Type 550

The racing and experimental departments were now in the new Werk II building and the project moved along quickly. Type 550 was the designation given to the ladder-frame sports car design begun early in 1953. The rear suspension crossmember was placed far back, and the radius arms reached forward, as in the Glöckler Specials and Porsche 356-001. Rear-wheel motion was damped by tube shocks and a large "rubber band" between each axle and a pulley on the chassis, which ran below. The new synchro transmission included a limited-slip differential from ZF, and most of the running gear was straight from the production cars. Notable exceptions

Carrera Panamericana, 1953

Juroslav Juhan, here shown before the start of the 1953 event in his special 550 coupe, won three legs of the race after the two factory Spyders went out, but a distributor gear broke and he ended up riding over a thousand miles to Mexico City along with his car on a farm truck. The biggest problem for most competitors was tire wear; even the light Spyders shed their Dunlop racing rubber after only a few hundred miles. All problems were overcome in 1954, however, when Juhan placed fourth overall after Hermann in a factory 550. Dave Friedman

were the hydraulic clutch and front-mounted oil cooler. Just ahead of the transmission was a 1500 Super engine with Solex 40 PII dual-throat carbs, now tuned for a power output of 98 hp on alcohol at a 12.5:1 compression ratio.

The aluminum bodies for the first two cars were built by Weidenhausen, with removable hardtops ostensibly designed to reduce wind resistance on a fast course. The finished machines were not particularly attractive, especially with hardtops in place, but they certainly looked like racers. At the end of May, the first of these was given its maiden run. Without a top in the pouring rain, 550-01 was driven to victory by Helm Glöckler in the Eifelrennen 1500 cc class at the Nürburgring.

This portent reinforced the company's determination and in June, the team headed for Le Mans. Chassis number 550-01 was driven by Helm Glöckler and Hans Herrmann, and 550-02 was shared by von Frankenberg and Paul Frère, a Belgian automotive writer. Engines for the cars were detuned to run on pump fuel, required by Le Mans rules, and at 9.0:1 compression returned about 77 hp. The tops were installed after some deliberation; it was felt they would enhance top speed, shown in practice to be around 124 mph on the Mulsanne straight. The cramped covering meant that drivers had to endure twenty-four hours inside a tin drum, but in spite of the discomfort and high engine oil temperatures, both cars outsped and outlasted their competition, with von Frankenberg and Frère taking a 1500 cc win and a new class record.

At the Avus track in Berlin, Helm Glöckler and Hans Herrmann had little luck in a July race. One of the cars was damaged in a spin, but repaired in time for a sports car race before the German Grand Prix at the Nürburgring on August 2, 1953. Herrmann won the 1500 cc class in both this event and at the Freiburg hillclimb a week later.

At this point, Porsche apparently felt that this particular chassis design could yield no more development benefits; the cars were refurbished and fitted with special equipment including an extra spare tire, louvered vents and increased air filtering and oil capacity. The duo was shipped to Guatemala where their new owner, Jaroslav Juhan, had entered them in the 1953 Carrera Panamericana. A Guatemalan, José Herrarte, drove chassis number 550-02 while Juhan, a transplanted Czech, piloted number 550-01. In typical fashion, the cars battled not only their competitors and the clock, but the wild roads and unexpected obstacles, from burros to boulders. Juhan's 01 soon dropped out, but Herrarte went on to a class win. The only other finisher in the under 1600 cc group was a 356 coupe driven by Fernando Segura of Argentina. Over the next year, these first 550s were put to the test again in races in Buenos Aires and Florida, and 550-01 made an encore at the

1954 Carrera Panamericana. In that race, its final event, the 550 actually turned in a better time than it had the year before, but finished fifth in class.

Type 550/1500 RS

A further refinement of the 550, drawing on experience gained in racing the first two cars, was already being constructed by early summer 1953. Still based on the mid-engine configuration, a revised ladder frame now placed the rear torsion bars ahead of the engine, similar to the switch made after 356-001, and the trailing arms were lengthened. The frame was arched *over* the rear axles and a bow-shaped engine-mounting cross-member, extending downward, was bolted in place rather than welded, to facilitate powerplant removal. Erwin Komenda scribed a new body that had more refined curves and rear fenders that ended in chunky fins, and these next few aluminum bodies were built by Weinsberg. The nose of car number 550-03 had a hood that curved down to an air inlet mouth. Four separate grilles were located on the rear deck and louvers were built into the sides behind the doors. On the next car, chassis number 550-04, a high rear deck was bolted in place for testing purposes, along with a full-width windscreen and small side windows.

The new engine designed by Ernst Fuhrmann was ready for installation in a vehicle, and when in July 1953, chassis number 03 was finished, an era began. At the Nürburgring on

The 550 chassis 04 with high back was shown at the Brussels Auto Show in January 1954. The knock-off wheels were not used on subsequent Spyders, since their light weight made frequent tire changes unnecessary. Porsche

August 2, young Hans Herrmann, who was now Porsche's number one driver, and von Hanstein both made a few practice laps but their times were disappointing. The elegant machine attracted interest among the spectators, but no one got a look under the hood. Those familiar with the 356 engine noticed a different exhaust note, though, and speculation intensified when the next week, Hans Stuck drove the car at the Freiburg hillclimb. Stuck was an acknowledged hillclimb ace, but he couldn't make the peaky engine work properly that day. Again the disappointed team kept the engine cover closed.

Chassis number 550-05 sported a new style nose, with a hood that was more conventional and at the rear, a single grille and revised "fins." Appearing as a road car with a real windshield and wipers, folding top, two seats and even a glovebox, chassis number 05 was shown at the Paris Auto Show in October 1953, accompanied by the announcement that this new sports racer, the Type 550/1500 RS (Rennsport) with a four-cam engine, was available for sale to customers. The new powerplant was no longer a secret, but in reality, many more changes would be made before a "production" 550 was released.

While the public was getting an eyeful in Paris, the 550-03 and 550-04 cars were on their way to the United States. Porsche planned to enter the cars in the November 1953 Carrera Panamericana, with sponsorship from the California-based Fletcher Aviation company, which was using Porsche engines in its light jeep vehicle. The cars were fitted with pushrod engines and driven to Hamburg, then loaded on a ship for New York. Max Hoffman was anxious for some exposure on his side of the Atlantic, so the cars were also entered in an SCCA race at Turner Air Force Base in Albany, Georgia. Porsche had brought in the big guns—Karl Kling, who had won the previous year's Carreras Panamericana in a 300SL, was on loan from Mercedes, and Hoffman had arranged a large press reception in New York to show off the racing team. Kling was mistaken for a communist sympathizer of the same name, got caught up in customs red tape and missed the party, but was released in time for the Georgia race, although the whole group might just as well have stayed on Ellis Island. In Georgia, mechanical problems plagued both cars, and the Mexican adventure was still to come.

The fourth Carrera Panamericana was the first in which the factory was putting forth an effort, and von Hanstein had high hopes for his team. Kling described the 550 as "a beautiful car, easy to handle, with excellent road-holding, with a top speed of 200 kph even though it only had an output of 80 hp.... After the 300SL it was like a delightful toy." The Porsche Spyders dominated the first leg, but in the second, Kling broke a driveshaft and was given a lift by a passing competitor in an American sedan. Not far down the road they came upon Hans Herrmann whose steering had broken at 85 mph. Young Herrmann had carefully braked and stopped the car against a rock wall, a little worse for the wear. The race was over for both Germans, but Herrarte in a private 550, number 550-01, and Segura in a 356 coupe took honors as the sole finishers in the under 1600 cc class.

Back in Zuffenhausen, the high deck tried on chassis number 04 showed promise in wind-tunnel testing at Stuttgart Technical Institute, so a body was built to incorporate the shape, and in that form was shown at the Brussels Auto Show in January 1954. It sported the same knock-off wheels shown in Paris, but these were not used in racing; the car's lightness precluded frequent tire changes. Gordon Wilkins, describing the car on the Porsche stand for the 1954 *Annual Review of Automobiles*, said, "The body was built up behind the seats to improve streamlining, on the general principal that the fastest open car was a closed car with a small hole in the top." Called the "Humpback," this car also introduced a design element that would endure for years—a hinged rear body shell that allowed easy access to almost all of the mechanical components. The opening body shell was necessary now, since the chassis reverted back to underslung, running below the rear axles, although 550-08 saw the frame changed back to an arch

Next page
Sharing no components with the 356 pushrod engine, Ernst Fuhrmann drew the Type 547 engine on a clean sheet of paper. The radically oversquare design of 66 mm stroke and 85 mm bore allowed the engine to rev quite high, but at a cost of torque. A near-hemispherical combustion chamber was fed by 48 mm intake and 41 mm exhaust valves. These were operated by a complex set of shafts and gears, inspired by previous Porsche Auto Union and Cisitalia designs. A half-speed shaft running below the crankshaft (where the camshaft would be in a pushrod engine) was driven at the flywheel end. At its other end, this countershaft drove light, hollow shafts that extended out to the center of the head, where the exhaust camshaft was then driven, and the intake cam via another vertical shaft. These shafts were geared to turn at crank speed, twice as fast as the cams, allowing them to transmit power yet retain light, hollow construction, since they did double duty as oil-pressure lines to the heads. The first series of engines (as shown here) drove a distributor from the end of each cam, while later versions moved the distributors to the nose of the crankshaft where they were less susceptible to vibration. All in all, it was an ingenious design that required meticulous assembly and service, and though many mechanics cringed at the thought of working on it, the 547 and its successors brought Porsche into the victory circle many times in its dozen years of competition. Initial questions about the ability of an air-cooled engine to generate high power output had long since been laid to rest when the final version of the four-cam produced almost 200 hp. Porsche

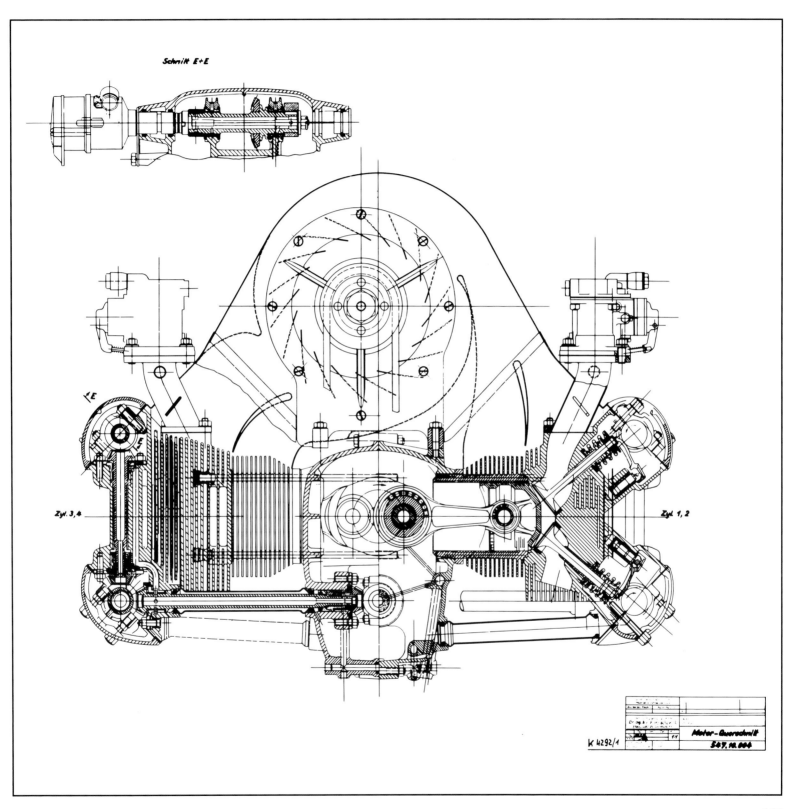

Schnitt E+E

Zyl. 3, 4

Zyl. 1, 2

K 4292/1

Motor-Querschnitt
547.12.004

over the axles. In April 1954, these two were thoroughly tested at Hockenheim, Germany, giving the factory enough confidence to enter one car in the upcoming 1954 Mille Miglia. The Type 547 engine used in Italy was already a second-generation unit, using Weber carburetors and with numerous detail changes.

Hans Herrmann was behind the wheel of chassis number 08 with Herbert Linge, the Porsche race department mechanic as co-driver, when they left Brescia on May 1 for 1,000 miles at speed on Italian roads. The race had its share of drama, including a quarter of an hour drying the ignition after a rainstorm. But the memorable moment came when the pair rounded a

sharp bend to find a railroad crossing gate lowering into their path with a locomotive bearing down on them. Without slowing, Herrmann slapped the top of Linge's helmet, though his navigator needed no incentive to duck as the low car roared under the crossing gate. The rest of the race, even the finish—sixth overall and winning their 1500 cc class—must have seemed anticlimactic. To many at Porsche, this "private-entry" success made Le Mans look like a sure thing.

Four cars were prepared for the French classic in June 1954. Three were equipped with third series 547 engines reflecting a number of small improvements and generating 114 hp at 6800 rpm on blended pump fuel. These cars carried rear

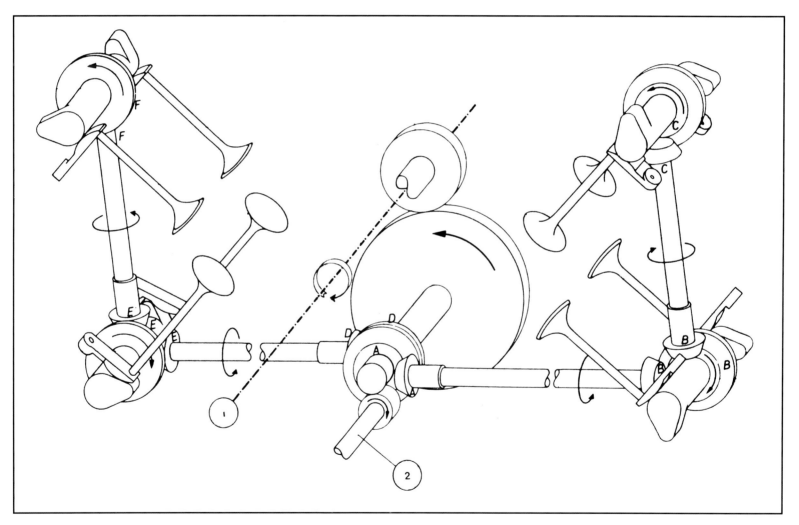

The elaborate cam drive in the Type 547 engine required proper adjustment of no less than six sets of bevel gears (A-F) not to mention end-play for each shaft and correct bearing and valve clearances. The crankshaft (1) turned the half-speed shaft that then turned the two camshaft drives and the oil pump shaft (2). Porsche

fender stripes in red (Herrmann and Polensky), blue and green. The fourth, with yellow stripes, was an entrant in the 1100 cc class, driven by Gustave Olivier and Zora Arkus-Duntov. Arkus-Duntov at the time was an engineer with General Motors where he was busy developing a new Chevrolet sports car, the Corvette. In Arkus-Duntov's Porsche, the small-displacement four-cam, with a bore of 72.5 mm, was producing just over 72 hp—enough to finish the race reliably, in fourteenth place, after every other car in its class had dropped out.

The large-engine 550s were having a rough go of it, however. The first to drop out, von Frankenberg and Helm Glöckler's car, was in the pits for good after only twenty-one minutes. In spite of cool, wet weather, improper ignition timing had caused overheating and put a hole in a piston. Twelve hours later, the red striped car was in with the same problem. As expected, Paul Stasse and Johnny Claes in the third Porsche suffered the same fate, but the mechanics were determined to salvage some chance in the 1500 class. The bad cylinder was deactivated, and the car plugged along on three for the last few hours. The only other cars left in the class, two OSCAs, were miles ahead, battling each other for the lead. Both went off a curve in the rain during the last hour of racing, allowing Porsche to back in to the class win, twelfth overall. The victories looked good on paper, but the engineers knew they had a lot more work to do.

That summer the racing department was kept busy modifying and preparing cars for competitions such as Rheims, France, where two 550s put in twelve hours and finished one-two in class. By August, engineer Helmuth Bott had created an airfield skidpad, based on suggestions from Arkus-Duntov. This new testing ground provided an effective means to sort out certain handling problems with the chassis. One major race was upcoming—a chance to show hundreds of thousands of spectators what the Porsches were made of—a sports car race that preceded the German Grand Prix at the Nürburgring. Herrmann, von Frankenberg, Polensky and von Hanstein started and finished the race in first through fourth places. At the Berlin Avus track in September, a streamlined variation on the body theme was tried for Herrmann, while von Frankenberg drove a normal 550. There was little appreciable difference in performance between the two siblings, and they both finished in front of the EMWs. Other venues produced similar results, and by season's end the four-cam engine was completely at home in the body for which it was designed.

Hans Herrmann capped the 1954 season by taking chassis number 04, now equipped with a four-cam engine of 117 hp, back to Mexico for the last Carrera Panamericana where he took third overall and the 1500 cc class title, thirty-eight seconds ahead of Juroslav Juhan. In the final standings of that class, an OSCA wedged itself into third place between the 550s of Juhan and Segura but the only other finishers were three other Porsches, number five being Salvador Lopez-Chavez in the veteran 550-001, sans top.

550 "Customer" Spyders

The first eight experimental 550s were joined by a number of others during 1954. Karl Ludvigsen stated that "estimates range from twelve to twenty-two Le Mans-type cars built *over*

With the Type 550 Buckelwagen are Ferry Porsche's sons: in the car, Wolfgang, standing from left, Peter, Gerd and Ferdinand Alexander, called "Butzi" in the family. Porsche

and above the original eight prototypes." The factory had a habit of re-bodying some chassis to meet new applications and selling off others as their usefulness decreased. But the end result was that the vehicle was sufficiently developed for series production. The apparent focus of the entire project was finally reached in the last months of 1954 when the Wendler coachbuilding firm, located in Reutlingen, supplied bodies for the first "customer" Spyders, as they were called. Max Hoffman insisted that the cars to be sold in America have a name, rather than a cold, impersonal number, and he christened them the Spyders. One could argue that the name Spyder is hardly descriptive of a fast, hot-blooded sports car, but the precedents existed both in the United States and in then-current Italian cars, where the name implied a light, quick, open roadster. Regardless of origin or spelling, the word quickly became part of the Porsche lexicon.

The production cars differed from their predecessors in a number of small ways. The aluminum used in the body was somewhat thicker and sheet steel was added at the bracing tubes behind the rear torsion bar tubes. At the front, the headlights were standard 356 units and running lights there and at the rear were a larger, circular design. A cockpit-actuated flap controlled the amount of air reaching the front oil cooler through a small grille. The rear fins were not so prominent, and no side louvers were used behind the doors, which were now slightly smaller. Civilianizing the car brought the dry weight to about 1,350 lb., more than ten percent heavier than the prototypes.

Even though it pulled a bit more weight, the four-cam engine, now in its fourth variation and called Type 547/1, still gave the kind of performance that could take a person's breath away, especially if that person were a passenger in a Spyder fitted with a small racing windscreen. The notoriously conservative factory spec sheets gave figures of 110 hp DIN at 6200 rpm, and 87.5 lb-ft of torque DIN at 5000 rpm. A 24 gal. tankful gave a front-to-rear weight balance of 48/52, and the stock 356 brakes could slow the light car as well as the engine could accelerate it.

Customers, as expected, quickly took to the tracks with their Spyders and the summer of 1955 was a banner year for the marque. Americans, especially West Coast enthusiasts like Richie Ginther and Ken Miles, were shimming their valve springs, increasing compression up to 12.0:1 and carb-swapping to get up to 130 hp. In March, a new Type 550 was driven at Montlhéry to six new 1500 cc class records by Walter Ringgenberg and von Frankenberg. Spyder drivers were not unbeatable, but they won the lion's share of races early in the 1955 season, including Le Mans, where 1.5 liter cars could make almost 140 mph on the straights. They took the first three places in their class and won index of performance, the first time for an engine of that size. Arkus-Duntov was back, this time with Auguste Veuillet as a co-driver, to take first in the 1100 cc class, followed by a privately entered Spyder. Aiding the Le Mans effort were new front brakes with drums widened by 20 mm, increasing lining area by one fourth with small brake cooling inlets in the nose.

Though the design was only a few years old, by the end of the 1955 season the Spyder's performance was being eclipsed by the competition. EMWs and Edgar Barth in a 1.5 liter Maserati were showing their tails to 550 pilots in Germany and in

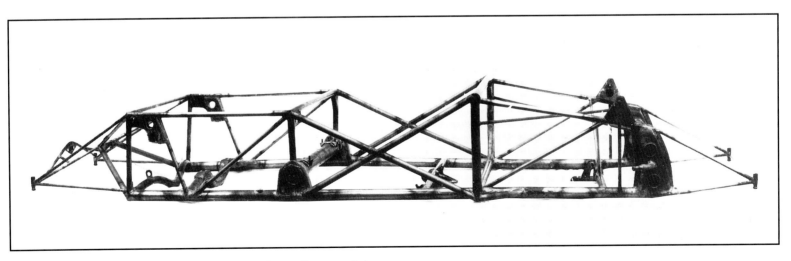

The 550A Spyder was built with a space frame but still retained the VW-style torsion bar front and rear suspension. Porsche

the United States, cross-bred "Poopers"—svelte Cooper bodies with Porsche engines—were making the Spyder owners look bad in SCCA races on both coasts. Pete Lovely of Seattle, Washington, built such a car using a 1500 S pushrod engine with a VW transaxle, and did well against California racers during that summer. In Max Hoffman's backyard, Gordon Lipe of Massachusetts was beating Hoffman's 550 customers in a similar car, and in 1956 the most potent Pooper of

all was built for John von Neumann with a new chassis and a four-cam engine.

In August 1955, the factory continued the Spyders' mechanical evolution with a five-speed transmission. In this new gearbox, the first gear was mounted along with reverse in the nosepiece. Unsynchronized and used solely for starting, it allowed the other four gears to be spaced closely and geared higher. At the Tourist Trophy event in Ireland on September

Continental Divide Raceway, Colorado, July 1960
Even Indy hero Rodger Ward campaigned a 550A, carrying an unusual all-American paint scheme denoting the Leader Card team and

naming the car the Sportor. The paint survived, but not the engine. A frustrated Ward sold the car soon afterwards. Dave Friedman

127

Riverside, June 1962
George Follmer at Riverside in a 1962 SCCA race. By this time the

550A was getting a little long in the tooth, but most cars still saw a lot of track action. Dave Friedman

22, the new gearbox failed and though the car finished, driven by von Frankenberg and Linge, the class win went to another factory 550 driven by Americans Masten Gregory and Carroll Shelby. A few days later another five-speed Spyder was entered at the Avus in Berlin. Von Frankenberg outlasted the EMWs on the high-speed track, and the car was then sent to Belgium where it set new 1500 cc speed records for that country.

By now the Spyder had made quite a splash in sports car circles, but at $5,800 *ex factory* and $6,500 in the United States, there was no chance of them ever becoming common. Some were regularly driven on the highways, often to and from races, including one of the cars sold by John von Neumann's Competition Motors in Los Angeles. It went to a young film star named James Dean who had been racing a 1500 Super Speedster, but wanted something faster. Driving from Los Angeles to a race in Salinas in September 1955, he was hit nearly head-on by an errant driver in a Ford and killed instantly. Riding with him was Rolf Wütherich, a factory mechanic who was in California instructing and troubleshooting for von Neumann and who survived the accident. Porsche received a great deal of dubious publicity as the wreck was paraded across the Southwest in a display sponsored by a

road safety organization. Months later, it vanished from a train car somewhere in Texas and was never seen again.

Most of these cars were not subject to the hazards of public highways, but the racetrack presented dangers of its own and the Spyder's tube frame made for quirky handling at times. Privateers would continue racing some of the seventy-eight Type 550/1500 RS Spyders sold in 1954–1956, but by the end of 1955 the factory was well into a new program that would replace the original with a new chassis and an improved engine.

550A/1500 RS

Three distinct problems in the Spyder were addressed by the factory at the same time, in late 1955. The "flexible flyer" handling of the original car was due to chassis distortion in both the longitudinal plane—flex along the fore-to-aft ladder beams—and torsional movement—a twisting of the entire assembly. The solution to this was actually a step backward to the original 356 design, a space frame made up of small tubes. The new chassis was carefully conceived and built from thin-wall tubing with each section stressed to produce an extremely strong unit. The result was three times the torsional strength and five times the longitudinal strength of the ladder

128

frame. With more panel attachment points, the weight of both chassis and body was down by almost 100 lb.

Front suspension remained much the same, but the rear was completely revised, based on a Mercedes-Benz application. The ubiquitous Porsche swing-axle suspension still used the transverse torsion bars, but was modified by lowering and centering the axle pivot point with separate lateral arms that pivoted from just under the transmission to the bottom of the trailing arm and hub assembly. New outer universal joints provided true independent rear suspension, and dramatically improved the earlier car's tendency to wag its tail in hard cornering.

The third improvement was in the engine, where Wilhelm Hild and the development engineers found that relocating the

Continental Divide Raceway, Colorado, July 1961
Bob Holbert and crew take advantage of plenty of parking lot space *for a clutch swap and some maintenance work on their RS 61.* Dave Friedman

129

distributors to the crankshaft nose gave much-improved ignition control and with 9.8:1 compression and Weber carbs, both power and torque output were up. Other detail changes were 12 volt electrics, a new ZF steering box, finned tube shock absorbers and a few body modifications. The hinged rear engine cover was now a lift-off unit with large louvered doors on either side for carburetor and oil tank access. The 550A weighed 1,166 lb. dry and would accelerate to 60 mph in 7.2 seconds, but these new models would not be available to the public until late in the year.

For the 1956 season, four examples of the improved version were successfully used by factory drivers, though the first outing in April at the Mille Miglia failed to impress anyone. Hans Herrmann was a back-marker in the Italian enduro, but that same car, driven by Count Wolfgang von Trips and Umberto Maglioli, and a second driven by Herrmann and von Frankenberg took first and second in class, fourth and sixth overall respectively at the 1,000 km Nürburgring race in May.

That contest had the potential for being a watershed event in motorsports history, but racing politics relegated it to footnote status. A young Swiss engineer named Michael May appeared in the paddock with his cousin Pierre driving a well-worn 550 Spyder that sported a curious appendage. A wing, mounted above the cockpit, was designed by May to increase the downforce on the tires at speed, augmenting grip in fast corners. Situated at the car's center of gravity, the device was adjustable from the driver's seat and in a rainy practice session, May was able to pass the best drivers in the fastest cars and his fourth-fastest qualifying time was better than either of the factory Porsches. It is understandable that von Hanstein pressured the organizers to disqualify May, using the argument that the device blocked the vision of other drivers. But it is hard to believe that neither Porsche nor any other competitors took any interest in what was clearly an extremely effective tool for increasing performance. Well over a decade would pass before the concept would again be applied to racing cars. Michael May went on to become an established engineer who would work for Porsche in 1961 and feature prominently in the development of the four-cam engine in its ultimate form.

Flushed with confidence in the new car after the one-two class finish at the 'ring, Maglioli and von Hanstein hatched an impulsive plan to enter the Targa Florio in Sicily. With a hastily-painted Spyder and only two mechanics, the pair decided only days before the June 10, 1956, race to try their luck on the tortuous island course.

The larger Ferraris and Maseratis were soon felled by mechanical problems and after eight hours of rough, twisting roads the Italian's solo drive paid off with a checkered flag for

Daytona, April 1959
The Von Dory 718 followed by an OSCA. Unlike many other sports

racers, Porsche never used center-lock wheels, as the car was generally easy on tires. Dave Friedman

the little white Porsche. The overall win was only the second for a German team since Dr. Ferdinand Porsche's 2.0 liter Mercedes won the Sicilian race in 1924. It was hailed as Porsche's greatest victory, though the factory's effort was, as Karl Ludvigsen describes it, "informal to the point of being ridiculous."

From the racing department in Zuffenhausen Werk I came two new cars for the June 1956 twenty-four-hour race at Le Mans. New regulations required full windshields, and again the roadsters were converted to coupes, this time by riveting a full roof to the removable rear cover panels. The enclosed shape was good for Mulsanne straight speeds of 138 mph in the rain and though one car retired, von Frankenberg and von Trips took class honors at fifth overall, second in the index of performance. The 1956 season continued with the first three places in the Rheims twelve-hour race, a one-two win at Solitude and a season finale with von Trips taking the class win on the long Avus oval in Berlin. Here, Porsche's success was overshadowed by their most spectacular failure, the results of pushing aerodynamic efficiency beyond the limit.

Type 645 *Mickey Mouse*

A new style Spyder, Type 645, was built as a logical extension of the ideas used so far in the 550 series. If light and small worked well, then lighter and smaller should be even better, though the truth in this reasoning remained to be seen. The vehicle, ready in July 1956, was some 5½ in. narrower and 4 in. shorter than its sibling, the 550A. Seen from above, its rounded nose, faired-in lights, covered passenger seat and rear-facing engine air ducts gave it a purposeful look. Underneath the magnesium skin an early-style four-cam engine was tightly enclosed, as were the tires and driver, for that matter. The single-seater had a fuel tank in the passenger's spot with other innovations like oil cooling lines running through ribs under the hood surface and a new twin-wishbone rear suspension.

Richard von Frankenberg was the only man to drive the car in its three public appearances and he gave it the name *Mickey Mouse* in recognition of its tendency to dart about at speed. Owing to a much smaller frontal area and light weight, the car's superior top speed would be an advantage on a course like the Avus, but handling problems remained even after transmission, braking and overheating defects were sorted out. In the September 16 German Grand Prix at the Berlin track, von Frankenberg was in the lead going into the steeply banked brick wall of the north curve when his car suddenly veered to the right, up the bank and over the wall. Hurtling through the air, he was thrown from the car and landed in bushes below where he was found, unconscious but unhurt,

minutes later. *Mickey Mouse* landed in a parking area and burst into white-hot magnesium flames.

Afterward, von Frankenberg did not remember the accident itself, and in his book, *Porsche, the Man and His Cars*, he devoted but a single paragraph to the project and its spectacular end. For their part, Porsche management was also quite willing to forget the car entirely, although certain features pioneered in *Mickey Mouse* were included in later models.

550A "Customer" Spyders

With the racing season ended, the 550A was now offered to customers, superceding the original Spyder. Thirty-seven were built in 1956 and 1957, many finding their way to the United States where they were consistent winners in SCCA racing across the country. Bob Holbert from Pennsylvania bought one, beginning a family connection with Porsche that would last for decades. The factory's policy was becoming clear by now: each sports-racing model would be made avail-

The interior of an RS60 illustrates the simple and functional approach taken by Porsche. A 10,000 rpm tach is the centerpiece of the stark, blackpainted dashboard. The hump over the instruments was considerably less pronounced than in the 550 series. In 1961, the fuse box was placed on the dash at right. Earlier cars were often seen with tan vinyl-upholstered seats, but red was more common later. Even updated for vintage racing, this Spyder retains much of the original uncluttered feel in the driver's area.

able to private buyers just about the time an improved version was ready for works drivers. By early spring 1957, a new incarnation of the Spyder was well under way, but some time would elapse between its first appearance and its readiness for battle.

Type 718 RSK

The ongoing struggle to control changes in camber during suspension movement led to a revision of the front torsion bars. The top tubes were moved higher and their centers canted downward, the four tubes now suggesting the letter K on its side when seen from the front. Thus, the Type 718 was commonly called RSK, though a revised frame that allowed

the cowl to be lowered by almost 5 in. and an elegantly streamlined body were bigger news than the front suspension. The frame was stronger and lower than its antecedent, and the body more slippery. Wind-tunnel testing had shown that the tail of the car was a good place to scavenge air for cooling, so the 718 had grilles in the seat of its pants. *Mickey Mouse* was not completely forgotten: faired headlights in the sloping, rounded nose and an integral hood oil cooler recalled that ill-fated short-wheelbase car. A replaceable nose panel could carry lights or ducts if necessary.

Another distinct body feature showed up after the car's first public appearance at practice for the Nürburgring 1,000 km race in May 1957. Instability was noted in both straights

Road America, September 1962
Bob Holbert's car, here at the Road America 500, clearly shows the
roll bar which was hidden under the headrest on most RS 60 and later cars. Dave Friedman

and corners, so when appearing at Le Mans the next month, square fins had sprouted on each rear fender. During practice a new factory driver from East Germany, Edgar Barth, made a spin of no less than eight revolutions, causing some concern about the fins' effectiveness. In the race, the car proved no faster than the previous 550As and crashed out before the halfway mark. Realizing that this was no contender, Porsche entered an RSK in only a few hillclimbs the rest of that season and began to sort out the problems.

Two new engines were added to the four-cam line-up by 1957, displacing 1587 and 1679 cc, but for convenience called the 1600 and 1700. The smaller of these, Type 547/4, had a bore of 87.5 mm while the 547/5 carried 90 mm barrels. New high-lift cams were effective, but ironically only when paired with American valve springs of higher quality than any available in Germany. First used in 2.0 liter hillclimb classes, these "large" four-cams later proved competitive with engines half again their size.

At the same time, another idea was pursued with the prospect of saving 8 hp by replacing the double-entry engine fan with a jet-cooling design. It intrigued Porsche engineers briefly but the system, developed by the Fletcher Aviation

people for their paratroop jeep, was tried and dropped. Ducting around the exhaust outlets allowed the hot gases to pull cooling air along with them, but the system's noise was such that no one could stand to be around a car so equipped. Fuel-injection experiments were also under way, but would not be put into use for a few more years.

The bodies were still hand-built at Wendler in Reutlingen, and the cars seemed to be getting lighter each year while power from the aging four-cam just kept climbing. Fuel was now fed through 46 IDM Webers and with up to 9.8:1 compression, the motors could be tuned for power or longevity but drivers were warned to keep revs under 7600 rpm. A new Hirth crank was on-line with larger main and rod journals, but its design weaknesses eventually became apparent.

With more work by spring of 1958, the RSK finally came into its own at the Targa Florio with a second-overall finish, Barth and Frenchman Jean Behra piloting. The suspension had again been revised at the front, where the K went back to an H and the ball joints tried in 1957 were also dropped. At the back, the torsion bars were discarded for the first time in any Porsche. Watt links and coil-over shocks located the rear hubs with new universal joints inboard. The spit-case transmission

Mosport, September 1962
Bob Holbert and his RS 61 strain to keep a lead on Innes Ireland in a

Lotus 19. Lighter British cars were slowly but surely elbowing into the Spyder's turf. Dave Friedman

was gone, the new Type 690 replacement being similar to the tunnel-case unit used on the production cars. An oil cooler was added along the left rocker panel with a scoop below and an oval outlet ahead of the rear wheel opening—a distinguishing feature of the 1958 cars, along with five slits in the side access panels.

The RSK's record during the 1958 season included highlights at Le Mans, where Behra and Hans Herrmann in a 1600 placed third while Edgar Barth and Paul Frère took 1500 class honors and a fourth overall, closely followed by a 550A in fifth spot.

A center-seat adaptation, built from the Barth/Frère Le Mans car to the Formula Two specifications that had been revived in 1957, was entered at Rheims with native favorite Jean Behra driving. The car proved faster than any of the Cooper, Lotus or Ferrari competition in this 1.5 liter Junior series. A second for Barth at Nürburgring and a Masten Gregory class win at Avus demonstrated Porsche's serious intentions in Formula Two.

When the season ended on the Continent, Behra went to sunny California and with the assistance of ace mechanic Vasek Polak, gave many West Coast racers a view of the RSK's tail with a fourth overall in the *Los Angeles Times* Grand Prix. That car stayed in the United States, the first of seventeen RSKs in the country with drivers who would dominate SCCA Class F racing for the next four years, and other classes as well, when displacement was sometimes changed by private owners. For these racers, the Spyder was an $8,000 ticket to the trophy stand and Porsche couldn't build enough of them.

By the beginning of the 1959 season, Zuffenhausen was ready with a new rear suspension, now incorporating double wishbones in a semi-trailing configuration. The visual effect

Riverside, October 1959
Ken Miles (50) and Jack McAfee (88) were regulars on the SCCA

circuit in 1959, seen here at the Times Grand Prix. RSK noses seemed to be particularly susceptible to dents. Dave Friedman

on handling was a lifting of the inside front wheel in corners, but the net result was softer springing and a bit more predictability. At Sebring, to kick off the year's racing calendar, Joachim Bonnier and von Trips in a Type 718 with the new rear suspension led Americans Holbert and Don Sesslar in a three-four-five Spyder finish behind the larger Ferraris with three more Porsches in the next six spots. Next outing, an excursion to Spa in Belgium, wasn't worth Paul Frere's effort but at Sicily's Targa Florio, the finishing order was Porsche one-two-three-four with Barth's 1.5 liter RSK overtaking the faster 1.6 when its transmission failed just short of the finish.

After a respectable showing at the Nürburgring, Ferry Porsche decided to wager all at Le Mans with high-lift cams in each factory car. That the decision was wrong became painfully evident as one after another of the Spyders retired with engine and drivetrain failures. Not a single RSK finished—the problems were traced to the larger-journal Hirth crank—but at least in this race the only victims were machines.

At the Avus five weeks later, factory 1500 RSKs were joined by private Spyder entries including Carel de Beaufort, who early in the race entered the bricks of the north banking too fast and could retain only enough control to steer over the top and bump his way down the other side through the bushes. He found himself in the paddock and, without hesitation, drove to the pit entrance and back onto the track where officials looked on in amazement while he rejoined the fray. After a few laps, the black flag came out for de Beaufort, but he had shown what a tough car the RSK was. Later in the race, Jean Behra was straining for the lead when his Spyder also slid up the brick banking, at a point where a concrete pylon was located, a gun mount left over after the war. His race and his life ended there, a great loss to both Porsche and Ferrari, with whom he had been under contract earlier that season. Von Trips won that tragic 1500 cc race, adding laurels to a season that would bring Porsche to a close third place in the sports car manufacturer's championship points with a near-miss at the last race in the series, the British Time Trial at Goodwood. There, von Trips' RSK outran Tony Brooks' 3.0 liter Ferrari in the last hour of this six-hour contest but could not catch Stirling Moss' Aston Martin.

With the end of the 1959 season, the Spyder had proven itself in six years of development as the machine to beat in everything from SCCA racing in the United States to European hillclimbs. At Le Mans, in Sicily's Targa Florio, at home on the Nürburgring and at smaller racecourses across the Continent, the point had been proven: this tube-frame aluminum-foil special with the unusual engine full of gears and cams could run with the big boys and leave them in the dust. Now perhaps it was time to set sights on a bigger prize—

Riverside, October 1959
Ricardo Rodriguez was the Mexican Wünderkind who, at 15, won his first race in a Spyder. Here at the Times Grand Prix in 1959 he was already a veteran of two seasons in a Porsche. "El Chamaco," as he was nicknamed, started out in motorcycles at the tender age of 11, and after getting a 550 as a fifteenth birthday present, would regularly challenge von Neumann and Ken Miles for the lead in 1500 cc classes. Here he is lined up in an RSK. Dave Friedman

Montgomery, New York, August 1960
Roger Penske and RSK on their way to the SCCA F Sports Racing
Championship in 1960. Dave Friedman

Riverside, October 1962
Bob Holbert graduated to an RS 61 and won the SCCA E Sports

Racing Class in both 1961 and 1962. The light metal nose shows the
effect of track debris. Dave Friedman

the Formula Two rules seemed to have been written with Porsche in mind. And from there, it wasn't that far a leap to the top, Formula One.

The direction taken by Zuffenhausen in the new decade would be toward Formula cars, though the RSK would live on.

The first Porsche open-wheelers took to the track in 1959, including the Porsche-Behra special based on the RSK. Initially, this Italian-built adaptation was more successful than the first of Porsche's F2 entries, but Zuffenhausen accelerated their efforts and by the beginning of the 1960 season,

Laguna Seca, October 1960
Bob Holbert inspects his state-of-the-art racing rubber on his RS 60 prerace at Laguna Seca. Standard rear wheel was a 15x4 in. unit carrying 6 in. section tires. Brake adjustment was made through the hub on the drum brakes, but Holbert got some of the first Porsche annular discs on a later RS 61. Oil tank and carb access were relatively easy through the louvered side panels. Dave Friedman

von Hanstein had secured the services of Stirling Moss and racing manager Rob Walker for the coming year and, they hoped, also for a venture into Grand Prix racing for 1961.

RS 60 and RS 61

For 1960, the RSK ran head-on into new regulations that mandated a close resemblance to "real" cars, including a higher windshield and even luggage space! Porsche's response was called the RS 60 and featured a wider body and a 4 in. longer wheelbase which, drivers agreed, improved handling. Fourteen were built, and customers didn't have to wait this year; for $9,000 a select few got the same cars as factory drivers. Newcomer Graham Hill and the team had a fairly successful season, highlighted by a victory in the Targa Florio but offset by a dismal placing at Le Mans to leave Porsche tied with Ferrari for manufacturer's championship points. The title went to the Italians, who had one more third-place finish.

Another fourteen Type 718 cars were built for the 1961 season and called, predictably, RS 61. It was another year of variations on a theme, including a stretched wheelbase on one open car, designed for an upcoming eight-cylinder motor. Two other chassis were used to build coupes, all three cars featuring a sharply raked nose and windshield, a new design by Butzi Porsche. Like the RS 60, the 1961 cars had built-in round

lights or horns at the front but the new cars had a large, front-hinged hood that extended below the nose. The initial race at Sebring, Florida, saw two factory cars drop out as Bob Holbert and Roger Penske brought home their customer RS 61 in sixth for the best Porsche finish.

A racing version of the 1966 cc four-cam production engine appeared in mid 1961, with plain bearings, a bore and stroke at 92x74 mm and the same 9.8:1 compression, producing 165 hp and better torque. It was used in the Targa Florio by Moss and Hill in the W-RS, the long-wheelbase roadster with a built-up full-width panel above the engine, louvered on its sides and open at the back, an adaptation of an appendage tried the year before. The English drivers were entered by the American Camoradi team, with close factory support, and Moss led the last lap until the transmission came apart, dashing hopes for a third straight Targa win. At Le Mans, the same car, now with plexiglass side windows, managed a fifth-place finish under Masten Gregory and Holbert, with the two factory coupes performing almost as well, though Jo Bonnier and Dan Gurney's coupe broke the clutch in the twenty-third hour.

At the end of the summer, Porsche could look back on a dismal season of competition. Development of the Type 753 flat-eight 1.5 liter Grand Prix engine, first begun in 1959, was maddeningly slow. The four-cam four was getting long in the

Riverside, October 1963
Richie Ginther was a Spyder veteran who had driven a von Neumann 550 and later, Formula 2 Ferraris and the Grand Prix Porsches. Here

he pilots an Otto Zipper RS 61 at the Times Grand Prix in October 1963. Dave Friedman

tooth and was beginning to be outclassed in endurance racing when Michael May came to Porsche from Mercedes in July 1961. By spring 1962, he was able to extract 185 hp from the 1.5 liter four, using Bosch mechanical fuel injection, a flat fan, and various head and piston modifications. His abrupt departure the next spring was related to internal politics at Porsche and coincided with the emergence of the eight-cylinder motor, which replaced the venerable four in endurance and formula racing.

Spyders had begun in 1953 as a direct descendant of the first Porsche and a close relative to the road cars, but after nine years of development, the thread of connection was stretched thin. The racing department by 1961 was busily engaged in the rarified atmosphere of Formula cars, but starting grids around the world were still filled with Porsches of all descriptions, from standard coupes to ultra lightweight specials. It was these road cars that carried on the spirit of the original Spyders with the last remaining link—the four-cam engine.

Laguna Seca, October 1960
Having spent the season in Porsche Formula cars, by October 1961 factory driver Joachim Bonnier was able to make an appearance at Laguna Seca in a less-than-pristine 718. Dave Friedman

Riverside, October 1962
At the Los Angeles Times Grand Prix in 1962, Bob Holbert does some bench racing as a crew works on Jack McAfee's RS 60. Number 11 was Jo Bonnier's W-RS that was on a tour of North American tracks in the last four months of the year. Prepared by Vasek Polak's Manhattan Beach shop, Bonnier was the fastest 2.0 liter qualifier at

Riverside, but the engine threw a rod after 23 miles. With a 200 hp Type 771 flat-eight cylinder engine and a six-speed transmission, the car should have been a contender. But neither Bonnier, Gurney or Holbert could consistently outrun the older Spyders that Autumn. Dave Friedman

Carrera Panamericana, 1953

At the 1953 Mexican road race, private owners joined the factory pushrod-engined Spyders. Salvador Lopez-Chavez was typical of Porsche's early customers: a wealthy shoe factory owner who had a competitive streak. Driving his 356 coupe number 151, he did not figure in this 1953 race, but in 1954 finished 5th in class and 28th overall in an encore appearance for 550 chassis 001. While the first race in 1950 was an almost all-American affair, the obvious superiority of Ferrari in 1951 set the stage for two classes in 1952, four in the next and five in the final Carrera in 1954. As a tribute to their class wins, the name lived on in Porsche's four-cam road cars. Dave Friedman

Chapter 11

Carreras

The Beauty and the Beast

The ultimate Porsche road cars took their very un-Germanic name from the Mexican Carrera Panamericana road races of 1952–1954 where production cars and the first Spyders tested their mettle against the clock and everything that one could imagine encountering on a road, including burros and vultures.

At the heart of the Carrera concept was the Type 547 four-cam engine, first tested in 1953, but not initially intended for use in a road car. When development first began, this sophisticated blend of cams, gears and roller bearings was planned as a pure racing engine in a vehicle that did not yet exist. But creating a car was easier than a complete engine; the 550 Spyder was ready before its powerplant.

The first "Carrera" was a coupe named *Ferdinand*, the car that was presented to the late professor on his seventy-fifth birthday and since his death, a test vehicle for new mechanical components. On its first outing with the 547 engine, the carbs caught fire and Ernst Fuhrmann had to extinguish them with snow, but Helmuth Bott and Ferry Porsche were impressed enough to send a 547 equipped Gmünd coupe to the Liège-Rome-Liège Rally in August 1954. Driven by Helmut Polensky, who had won the 1952 event for Porsche, with Herbert Linge as navigator, the 105 hp engine and light body proved an unbeatable combination in the four-day ordeal.

356 Speedster and 356A Carreras

A run of 100 production cars was authorized, just enough to homologate the model for Grand Touring racing under FIA rules. The new car was designated 1500 GS, carrying the same 547/1 engine as the Spyder but with slight changes in compression and a different distributor location. The Spyder's flywheel was toward the rear of the car with distributors extending from the inlet cams in that direction. Fuhrmann

must have anticipated a road version when he designed placement of the ignition drive at either end of the cam, and in the road car it was on the fan belt side of the engine.

With a proper muffler and 9.0:1 compression, horsepower was down to an even 100 at 6200 rpm, but did not drop off much even to 7000. Torque of 87.6 lb-ft was not reached until after 5200 rpm, but it was better to keep the engine turning in the upper ranges, anyway. The roller bearings definitely did

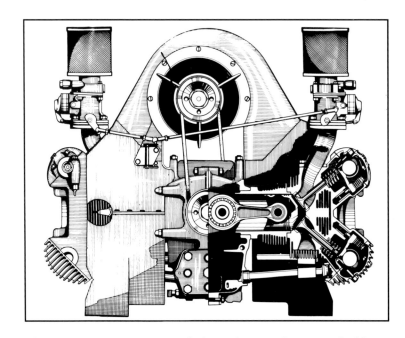

The four-cam engine was a tight fit in the rear of a 356, and adding a dry-sump oil tank and cooler made matters worse. Owners found that the easiest way to tune up an engine was to just take it out.

141

not like lugging and the plugs would foul with too much idling. An oil tank for the dry sump was placed in the rear of the left fender, with a filler inside the engine compartment. Spark plug access was problematical to say the least—changing eight plugs that you could not even see might consume the better part of an afternoon, even with the special tool supplied with each car.

Offsetting that frustration was the pleasure of driving the car. Old Porsche hands noted that in the mid 4000 rpm range, where the pushrod engine's power was starting to drop off, the Carrera was just beginning to build up steam. The exacting

Riverside, June 1962
Jay Hills in a Carrera holds off Ron Bucknum in a Ferrari 250GT long-wheelbase berlinetta at Riverside. With a 3.0 liter, 250 hp V-12 engine, the Ferraris were often overall race winners—but not always.
Dave Friedman

142

tolerances of the gear-driven valve system allowed smooth operation at engine speeds unheard of in the other Porsche engines. Jesse Alexander, writing in *Sports Car Illustrated*, related a 1959 test: "in most of our test runs we limited the revs to 6500 through the gears, but then upon returning to the factory we were given a short ride with Huschke von Hanstein, Porsche racing manager. We complained slightly about the car's performance so all he did was take the revs up much higher than we dared. 7000 rpm in first, and in second and third the needle just went off the scale, sailing up to where 8000 should be! Even at unspeakably high revs, we were impressed at the lack of that mechanical banging and chattering that one hears on pushrod Porsches when overstretched." The first three gears would bring the car to almost 90 mph with standard BBAA gearing, though the magic 200 km/h (124 mph) figure was not quite reached in the early production versions.

The Carrera entered the Porsche line-up concurrent with the introduction of the 356A in September 1955 at the Frankfurt Auto Show. Karl Ludvigsen wrote, "The Carrera was the inevitable Porsche, the car the Zuffenhausen enthusiasts had to build sooner or later." With larger tires and a dual-outlet exhaust that peeked out below the rear apron, the car projected a businesslike attitude, and with gold Carrera script gracing the sides and rear, this was obviously no ordinary Porsche. The first customers were divided among those "damn the amenities, full-speed ahead" competitors and others who took issue with the idea that the $5,995 automobile was not equipped with a heater.

In 1957, Carrera production was channeled into two distinct lines to appease both camps. In the Deluxe version, heat exchangers made it an all-weather automobile, similar in other details to the standard coupes and cabriolets. For the competition-minded, no such frills were needed. Their version, called the Grand Turismo (GT) in coupe or Speedster form, got light bumpers, larger 60 mm wide front brakes from the Spyder and a 21 gal. fuel tank. Door trim was rudimentary, including a leather strap to lower the plexiglass windows, and most GTs came with Speedster bucket seats. A 110 hp engine with optional Weber carburetors made its presence known to all through a sports muffler, and inside the car the bevel gear-and-exhaust rasp symphony was unfettered by insulation or undercoating. Here was a serious car for racers in the 1.5 liter classes, and soon enough, the 1.6 and larger categories as well.

Rolf Goetze brought his specially prepared 1529 cc Carrera Speedster to Monza in March 1957, where a twenty-four-hour record attempt was made in the 2.0 liter class. Averaging 116 mph, it broke 1,000 mile and 2,000 km records, retiring soon afterward but not before posting a best lap of almost 128 mph. Shortly thereafter, at the Marathon de la Route, which was fast becoming a Porsche playground, Claude Storez won the rally outright in a Carrera Speedster, beating a Mercedes 300SL. He then added to his season total with a fifth in the Tour de France that year. Private Carreras were showing up in all kinds of racing and doing well on either gravel or asphalt.

With the T-2 body changes came a revamped GT that featured doors, lids and seat frames of aluminum. The rear deck lid was louvered on either side of the standard grille, and cold-air ducting fed the carbs directly.

A factory coupe won the 1600 class at Sebring in early 1958, driven by von Hanstein and Linge. Its 5.167:1 rear-axle ratio gave startling acceleration, apparently well suited to the rough Targa Florio course in Sicily where it won the class that spring, again driven by Porsche's racing director, along with Baron Pucci. That car had an external oil cooler, and a few other changes that marked the first interim 1600 Carrera engines.

A combination of events had led to the development of an entirely new engine for the Carrera in 1958. The FIA had officially adjusted class limits to 1600 cc. Klaus von Rücker took the opportunity to not only increase the Carrera's bore to 87.5 mm, but to get rid of the roller crank, a sometimes troublesome element for owners who didn't exercise proper care. Given the type number 692/1, the new 66 mm stroke forged and counterweighted crankshaft gave a displacement of 1587 cc. The engine case was adapted to hold the new plain-bearing unit, and other improvements like sodium-filled exhaust valves and front oil coolers reflected experience acquired with the Spyders. Of particular importance was the repositioning of the distributor drive to the nose of the crank, just as the Spyder engine had previously been improved.

By mid 1958 the Carrera Deluxe had the plain-bearing engine, already in its third-generation, Type 692/2, and consideration was given to its use in all kinds of weather. Heat tubes kept the carbs warmed, and a gas-fired heater in the car's tail kept the driver warm. Solex 40 PII-4 carburetors, a diaphragm spring clutch and an optional limited-slip ZF differential were other changes. The ZF unit was an unusual design of jelly-bean-shaped bearings that rode between two plates with radiating ridges. It was effective, but like the roller-bearing crank, was prone to a short life if not treated properly. By now the mid-range 4.86 final-drive ratio was dropped and the 4.43 gears remained standard. Hillclimbers could still get the 5.17 stump-puller differential but with it, top speed was down to only 95 mph at 7500 rpm.

When the four-cam Carrera engine was offered as an option in the 1956 models, the combination of light weight and

The cockpit of a Carrera was significantly different from a pushrod-engined car. The 8000 rpm tachometer and 160 mph speedometer were a clue to what was in the engine compartment, and separate switches for each of two fuel pumps and ignition coils gave the dashboard a distinct and businesslike appearance. With minimal soundproofing, there was hardly any point in having a radio. On the plain door panels, a leather strap allowed the plexiglas windows to be raised or lowered. This 1957 1500 Carrera was shipped to Bangkok, Thailand, but made its way to the United States early in its career.

power made the ultimate Speedster. The 1958 Carrera GT models used aluminum in the doors, deck lid and seat frames in addition to a two-part wheel with aluminum-alloy rims and hubcaps.

This potent welterweight was made in small numbers through 1959, the last year's production outliving the rest of the Speedster line. Thirty-two of the 1959 Carrera GT models were produced; twenty-five GTs had four-cam engines, these being the first production Porsches with 12 volt electrics. The remaining seven GT Speedsters were fitted with 1600 Super pushrod engines. Of these, a sequentially numbered group of four were delivered to the Block dealership in Oakland, California. These four silver cars were ordered with unusual gearing and an incredible 6:31 ring-and-pinion ratio, giving them the potential for quick acceleration and even quicker engine over-revving.

The year 1959 appeared to be the end of not only the Speedster, but the entire Carrera line. No four-cam was in the road-car catalog when the new B model was introduced for the

1960 model year. The Super 90 satisfied some would-be Carrera customers, but in the end the racing enthusiasts were not forgotten after all. Some forty lightweight coupes were built in 1960-1961 with the 1600 692/3 and /3A engines; the factory had all but given up on the Deluxe customers, for the time being.

Trophy Chasing in the United States

In the United States at the end of the 1950s, the Carrera was the car to beat in a number of racing classes. Even when classification was changed and the four-cam was lumped in with Jaguars and Aston Martins, they continued winning at the hands of masters like Bruce Jennings. But the Sports Car Club of America (SCCA) seemed intent on making life difficult for Porsche and its American race customers. By 1961, the Carreras were allowed to use the new 692/3 engine with Weber carbs, 9.8:1 compression and 12 volt electrics. But they were bumped to B-Production where the Corvettes with twice their horsepower allowed them no higher than fifth place at season's end. In 1964, the classes were shuffled again and Carreras were once again in front. Bruce Jennings took 1964 honors in C-Production, and Dick Smith did the same in 1966. But by that time there was a new force to be reckoned with—the 911.

The success of Porsche in the new world did not happen without support from the factory. Max Hoffman was an enthusiastic promoter, and on the West Coast Johnny von Neumann's track exploits were an example to all of his competition-minded customers. While the pushrod engines were close kin to the VW that was fast becoming a fixture on American roads, in the mid 1950s the four-cam engine was still a piece of exotica that few mechanics would attempt to repair or even tune. A young man named Vasek Polak, a former motorcycle racer in his native Czechoslovakia, came to New York to work at Max Hoffman's agency. With his mechanic's earnings he bought a new Spyder and soon afterward headed to the West Coast where he developed a reputation as an ace mechanic, one of the few who could really make a four-cam engine scream. In December 1959, Polak opened the nation's first all-Porsche dealership in Manhattan Beach, California.

At the same time, Porsche had its own support network for racers. Troubleshooters were sent by the factory to the United States, each covering a specific area. In Hermann Briem's case, that was everything west of the Mississippi. He and Herbert Tramm in New York set up service schools to train mechanics in the proper Porsche procedures. Another responsibility was helping out with race preparation and trackside support at races around the country. The job meant crossing the country and crossing paths with club racers, professional drivers and even movie stars like Steve McQueen, who drove a black Speedster. Many racers developed their own tuning and building skills but for most owners, this personal factory support was a welcome touch.

Abarth Carrera GTL

Back on the Continent, Porsche was engaged in the struggle to stay ahead of the pack in the FIA Grand Touring categories. Since the rules allowed a different body from stock, the factory solicited bids from both Wendler, the Spyder builder, and Zagato, an Italian firm that just happened to build many of the competition's cars. Zagato's offer best met its needs, but the Porsche staff thought it might be unseemly to deal directly with the company that made the cars they wanted to beat.

Once again, Carlo Abarth became an intermediary, just as he had with the Cisitalia, this time lending his name and organizational skills. His shop assembled and tested the aluminum product of this alliance between Porsche, Zagato and Franco Scaglione, a designer and engineer who gave the new car an efficient, aerodynamic shape. Built on a B chassis and with a passing resemblance to the 356, the car was more than 5 in. lower, and almost as much was cut from its width. Aluminum construction resulted in a weight of 1,780 lb., 100 lb. less than a comparable steel Carrera GT.

The first GTL, as it was called, showed that more work was needed—no one could comfortably fit in the cramped driver's seat. The second car was good enough to win its class

Pomona, California, July 1962
The Speedster Carrera was a favorite on short, twisty courses where its light weight and short gears were an advantage. At higher speeds on long straights, it had the aerodynamics of a brick in spite of the rear cockpit fairing shown here. Dave Friedman

in the Targa Florio "right out of the box" in early May 1960 at the hands of Paul Strähle and Linge. Again at Le Mans, Linge copiloted a GTL to eleventh overall, first in class.

A new engine for the Abarth Carrera came on-line for 1961, with larger main-bearing journals and higher-lift cam lobes. Designed to rev higher, it was found that the geartrain floated at just more than 7000 rpm. It turned out that the new cams needed flywheels on their end to smooth out their high-rev resonance. The exhaust cams carried two flywheels apiece and the inlet cams one, a distinctive feature of the Type 692/3A engine. Solex 44 PII-4 carburetors were fitted, and with the Sebring exhaust it could put out 135 hp at 7400 rpm, with 107 lb-ft of torque at 5800 rpm.

In 1961, the GTLs kept the Porsche banner flying high with class wins at the Targa Florio and respectable finishes in a number of races that year and the next. In 1962, some of the twenty GTLs built went into private hands and were campaigned until the first plastic Porsche, the 904, came along in 1964.

Carrera 2

In September 1961, the Frankfurt Auto Show was again the launching pad for a new model, this time a 356 with a larger engine, the Type 587, dating from Ernst Fuhrmann's tenure six years before. This 1966 cc powerplant carried a 74 mm stroke crankshaft in plain bearings that just fit in the case, and 9.5:1 compression. Extending the cylinders, shafts and

tubes to accommodate the longer stroke made the engine 2 in. wider, but the new head shape allowed easier valve adjustment. Incorporating many of the changes made during the four-cam's lifetime, it made 130 hp at 6200 rpm, matched with 119 lb-ft of torque at 4600 rpm for the most flexible Carrera yet. Karl Ludvigsen stated, "The Carrera 2 was the first plush, fully trimmed, road-going Porsche that was capable of consistently breaking the ten-second barrier from rest to 60 mph."

For some time Porsche had used both drum brakes and annular ring discs of their own design on the racing machines. When the 356B 2000 GS was introduced in September 1961, drums were fitted, but by the time production got under way in April 1962, the annular discs were standard on the car and customers were warned that they should be warmed up before hard use.

The Carrera 2 was built in Deluxe versions of both coupe and cabriolet and the original goal of FIA homologation with 100 cars was reached after only four months. Eventually, 310 were built on the B chassis and with the introduction of the C, another 126 came off the production line, with the new Dunlop-Ate discs.

2000 GS/GT

While these civilized road cars were plying the highways, two race cars that shared their engine and chassis were terror-

Del Mar, California, April 1962
Whether a Carrera was passing or being passed by a Corvette often depended on how twisty the course was. Here Jay Hills negotiates a hard right-hander at Del Mar. Dave Friedman

Sebring, April 1962
The Abarth Carreras, homologated 356Bs, were lined up for the start of the Sebring endurance race in 1962. Number 49 was the Edgar Barth/P. Ernst Stahle mount; behind it was the Dan Gurney/Bob Holbert car, which won its class, placing 7th overall. The GTLs had bodies that were nowhere near the Porsche standards for weather-tightness, fit or finish. But even in the rain with gunwales awash, they were fierce competitors. Porsche

izing the tracks. The 2000 GS/GT competition coupes were ostensibly simple race versions of the B Carrera 2, but the Stuttgart-built aluminum-bodied cars had only a passing resemblance to the road cars. The shape, penned by Ferdinand Alexander Porsche, was similar to the RS 61 coupe, though that was a Spyder derivative with mid-engine and tube frame. Nicknamed the *Dreikantschaber*, or "triangular scraper," the two 2000 GS/GT examples that were built proved to be worthy contenders in many contests through 1964, when the 904 entered the GT arena.

Type 904 GTS

The Carrera 2 engine in racing trim, Type 587/2, could put out as much as 170 hp and almost as much torque. A final version of the four-cam motor, Type 587/3, was officially rated at 180 hp while turning 7200 rpm and 145 lb-ft of torque at 5000 rpm, all this with racing exhaust as fitted to the last of the Carreras, the GTS or Type 904. This car had no body or

chassis ties to the 356 line, but was a new generation of automobile, successful in its own right, following the tradition of excellence set down by its predecessors. The same could be said for its designer, the eldest son of Ferry Porsche who created a fiberglass body that turned heads like no other Porsche had ever done. The 904 was a bridge of sorts between the old generation and the new. The last of the four-cylinder engines was putting out almost 200 hp and before the 911 replaced it, the 904 carried six- and even eight-cylinder engines, a harbinger of things to come.

The year 1965 marked the end of an era for Porsche and the four-cylinder, four-cam engine. After a dozen years of development it had doubled in power and during that time had made the words Porsche and racing almost synonymous. The Carrera name would continue to be used to delineate the fastest of the Porsche road cars, but in their first decade, it had only one definition: a high-strung, barely civilized engine that turned "that funny little German car" into a giant killer.

The 904, designed by Ferdinand Alexander Porsche, carried its fiberglass body on a frame of two rectangular-section rails made of sheet steel, joined by cross-members at a number of points. Designed to use the four-cam four or the new six, later versions even had an eight-cylinder engine. Porsche

Epilogue

More than a quarter century after the last of 76,000 356 Porsches left the factory, the question is sometimes heard, "How many are left?" The answer is unclear, but estimates from a number of knowledgeable people put the figure at around one third of the original series still in existence. Natural attrition took many of them, but for many years they suffered the fate of "ordinary" cars: abuse, neglect and ignorance. At the end of its production run, the 356 was considered obsolete by most people. The new 911 provided more power and better handling in a modern package, albeit at a considerably higher price. It was this price gap that allowed the 356 to hang on for its last year or so, and the raison d'être for its immediate successor, the 912. When the low-line mantle was then passed on to the 914 and later, the 924, there was considerable unrest among those who did not consider these to be real Porsches, an attitude that made the old 356s that much more attractive.

By the mid 1970s, there was a revival of sorts, a recognition of the unique qualities of the car by more people than ever before. And best of all, these old bathtubs were affordable. If they had ever seen a winter, they were probably rusty, and chances are, they had not been driven by a little old lady. But these were real live Porsches—not swoopy 911s, but cars that you could relate to. Compared to the boxy, boring and anemic American iron crowding the post-oil-embargo highways, they were positively wonderful.

With the 1980s came a nostalgia fever that in mid-decade saw interest in the cars at an all-time high, and prices at a similar level. By the beginning of the 1990s, Carreras cost as much as a nice house, Speedsters were going for twenty times their original price and finally, the early cars got some of the attention they had so long deserved. The true enthusiasts, those whose affection for the 356 had never dimmed, were

In a market where demand for Speedsters and Spyders outstrips supply by a wide margin, reproductions abound. Beginning in the early seventies with a host of crude and often ugly VW-based "sports cars," copies of the Stuttgart thoroughbreds have evolved to a point where it is often hard to tell them from the genuine article at a distance. This Spyder replica, seen fueling up for a parade lap of Road America in Wisconsin, was built by a now-defunct Mexico City firm. Under the fiberglass shell is a VW engine with a custom fan housing that even looks like a four-cam engine. Its well-finished appearance is the result of a year's worth of detailing to the original completed kit. Another 550 facsimile is produced in California by Chuck Beck who offers either a kit or completed car. Beck's cars weigh about the same as the originals, and with a tweaked 140 hp VW powerplant, they can hold their own with anything on the street. Ersatz Speedsters are generally built on a shortened VW pan, while Spyders rely on a custom-built tube frame. The proliferation of these replicas along with a renewed interest in restoring originals has increased the number of reproduction parts available, to the benefit of both purists and repro builders.

taking renewed pride in their cars and making a dedicated effort to preserve the breed.

Owners clubs around the world have celebrated the marque for years, and in the United States, the 356 Registry holds semi-annual Holidays, mails a quarterly magazine and functions as a connecting point between 356 fanciers. Similar organizations exist in Europe, Japan and Australia with the result that, far from being a cold museum piece, the original Porsches can be seen today on racetracks, at concours d'elegance competitions and out on the road just for the fun of it. The meticulous detail of concours cars is sometimes offset by other 356s whose weathered appearance shows more regular use. Parked next to each other at a recent Registry Holiday were two Speedsters, each carrying a sign on their windshields. The card on the pristine example read, "Do not touch this car unless you are in the nude!" The other, a particularly

When it last raced, this 1958 Porsche won a national championship.

P.A.P. EP

(That was 6 weeks ago.)

Thirty years later, a lot of people are still following the Porsche 356 Speedster.

On October 15 some of America's best sports car racers followed one, as Joseph Cogbill's 1958 Speedster carried him to the 1989 SCCA E-Production National Championship.

While most famous cars of its era are collecting dust in museums, Porsche Speedsters are still collecting laurels on racetracks around the world.

So what kind of person puts a rare, extremely valuable classic car through hairpin turns in high-speed traffic? Anyone who knows anything about Porsches and the way they're built.

PORSCHE

Old Porsches are often used in television, movies and print advertising. Speedsters and Speedster replicas have co-starred in a number of Hollywood productions like Coming Home, 48 Hours and Top Gun. In magazines, models can be seen leaning on 356s selling everything from jeans and perfume to fried chicken. Mazda even used a Speedster to lend the proper atmosphere in a Miata promo and in this print ad, Porsche used an old Porsche to sell new Porsches. Though the ad may seem a bit whimsical, the facts are straightforward. Joe Cogbill has been at the top of the heap in SCCA E Production for a few years and every indication is that he will stay there—in a 1958 Speedster. Fallon/McElligot Agency

At swap meets, the prices go up as the number of items goes down. Even ancillary items like license plates, literature and models are in demand among 356 fanciers.

tired-looking veteran, had a hand-lettered note warning, "Do not touch this car unless you have had a recent tetanus shot!" Which car was driven hundreds of miles home? Both of them.

The ranks of modern-day 356 enthusiasts cover all age groups and a wide spectrum of individual interests. At opposite poles are the racers, often using heavily modified body and mechanical parts, and the concours crowd, who can distinguish an unoriginal bolt at twenty paces. But that is not to say they do not complement each other; many of the nicest show cars can be seen at autocross events and the best of the racers are meticulously prepared not only mechanically, but aesthetically. Today, a small number of SCCA competitors carry on a tradition that dates from the mid 1950s: Porsche 356s in the winner's circle. Vic Skirmants travels across most of the country from his shop in Michigan to compete in E- and F-Production classes. Joe Cogbill is a second-generation Porsche enthusiast who has been a consistent front-runner in E-Production for a decade. His Speedster, with a 160 plus hp pushrod engine, exhibits performance beyond what even the factory could have imagined thirty years ago. The fact that such a dated design is still competitive is the result of meticulous preparation and another Porsche tradition—good drivers.

While a good number of original owners still drive and enjoy their cars, many of the most fervent enthusiasts discovered Porsche 356s long after they had been relegated to used-car status. A case in point is Harry Pellow, who in the early 1970s was just another transplanted Californian driving from gas station to gas station in a thirsty Corvette. Tiring of the cost, he bought a Volkswagen and soon discovered, like so many before him, that he really liked the car. What he did not enjoy was the VW's tendency to eat exhaust valves, and when a friend suggested a Porsche, which was similar but stronger, Pellow got one. His first Porsche engine rebuild was not so complicated as he was led to expect, and after a few more rebuilds for friends he developed a reputation for thorough work. His curiosity about the many variations in engine parts from year to year led to his writing a book that delineates all the many permutations of the 356 powerplant. That first book was followed by a number of others that, along with a set of engine-assembly and tune-up videos, have informed and entertained many 356 owners. As a combination engineer, mechanic, critic, author, computer programmer, historian, social commentator, salesman, publisher, video star, political analyst and teller-of-talltales, Pellow is without peer.

About the time Pellow was discovering Volkswagens, Dave and Dennis Aase were fixing and reselling them in Newport Beach. They ended up with a used B coupe that was taking up space on a dealer's back lot, but soon the same dealership's bodyshop, where Dave worked, was asking if the Porsche had

Harry Pellow and a Maestro-massaged engine: rebuilt, powder painted and gold plated.

this part or that part. Eventually selling most of the car back to the dealership piecemeal, they discovered that the whole is *not* greater than the sum of its parts. By the mid 1970s they had their own Porsche salvage yard and were buying not only cars, but quantities of parts from European suppliers who just wanted to get rid of "that old junk." Ten years later much of that same old junk had made yet another trans-Atlantic crossing as the demand for 356 parts grew in Europe. Dennis also tells of the 1,400 or more stripped bodies that went off to a landfill over the years—but not anymore. Today the racks of valuable used parts are neatly arranged in the Aase warehouse, complemented by new reproductions of other 356 parts.

Though many of the unusual and unique parts will probably always be hard to find, more common items like sheet metal and trim have been reproduced for years. Some of these are second-generation bits, often indistinguishable from the originals. Brett and Peter Johnson built a thriving business in Indianapolis from an inability to find parts when they were fixing up old Porsches in the early 1970s. Brett's taste in transportation during high school ran along the lines of a Lotus 11 and a 1957 Porsche cabriolet—exotica today, but in 1972 just used cars, and strange ones at that. Graduating to both college and 911s, he became well versed in the peculiarities of each of the models and soon got to know the weak points of the 911, such as heat exchangers. While studying in England, Brett turned up a supplier of replacement heater units there and recognized an opportunity to sell them in the United

States. The brothers then collaborated in a business venture that grew to include rubber parts, metal body panels and, eventually, most of the replacement items needed for any model Porsche. Their company joined the ranks of specialty parts dealers who were marketing by catalog mail order, which has now become one of the most common means of buying Porsche pieces.

Brett's interest in the early cars has extended to the publication of a book detailing changes in the 356 models from year to year. A second edition has expanded on the information presented in the first, and has been joined by similar books covering the 911 and 914 series. After years of research, Brett and a host of other dedicated enthusiasts have made some sense out of the many changes in the 356 line. The factory itself was not known for explicit record keeping, especially in the early days when volume was low and the company's organization was less formal. Today, in addition to readily available parts, there is probably more good statistical information available than ever before. Of particular interest to the restorer with an eye to authenticity, the existence of these facts and figures is also important in the preservation of the marque.

Through much of the 1950s there were numerous items on the 356 that could be interchanged with Volkswagen parts, and Porsche ownership on a budget meant learning to read the VW parts manual upside down while standing at the local

dealership's service counter. While many of these VW parts from the 1950s have been no easier to find than a similar Porsche piece, a resurgence in interest among owners of older Beetles has given repro parts manufacturers a larger target market. Demand for some popular reproduction items like open-center chrome wheels has brought down the price for owners of both cars. But interchangeability has its downside: VW customizers using 356 engines and brakes are tapping a finite resource, at least until the cost of doing so becomes prohibitive.

In every facet of the conservation effort, individuals have taken the lead in providing information, parts and support for other 356 owners, but after all these years even the factory is now offering vintage parts. Where plastic filler and bodyshop paint used to be good enough, the restoration of these cars is now generally undertaken with an eye to authenticity, although some people are building what they think Porsche should have built in the first place. In California, Gary Emory sells obsolete parts and often engages in some whimsical creations; variations on a theme that are not quite original, but always crowd-pleasers.

Going even farther afield, there are reproductions of both the Speedster and 550 Spyder available in fiberglass. Unlike some of the VW-based atrocities that passed as kit cars in the 1970s, it is now possible to build your own vehicle and recreate at least some of the original car's personality: wind in the hair and a second look from pedestrians. And while few reproduction cars feel like limousines, the originals did not either.

The Midwest was the birthplace of the 356 Registry, and the Porsche Club of America originated on the East Coast, but California remains the center of interest for year-round Porsche fans. Type 356 repair shops are not uncommon, but at Jim Wellington's you will find only the rare and unusual. Rennsport Werke is the home of the four-cam. In this shop it takes an entire table to hold a disassembled Hirth crankshaft. Arranged in orderly containers of roller bearings, cages, journals and crank throws, the overall impression is of an intricate puzzle with no picture for reference. The 547 engine and its derivatives were always rare, and so few are left now that even exploded crankcases are brought back to life. It is neither easy nor cheap, but hopefully men like Jim Wellington and the owners of old Carreras will not let the distinctive exhaust note of a four-cam engine fade off into museum status.

With renewed interest in the entire 356 series, and the dedication and energy of those who, as Harry Pellow says, "Keep the 356 faith," we will continue to see the original Porsche sports car, the dream of a father and son, enjoyed and appreciated for generations to come.

These may be wrecks, but this is no junkyard. Dennis and Dave Aase preside over a business that has become a prime source for parts that are no longer available anywhere else.

Appendices

356 Specifications and Serial Numbers

The following lists have been compiled over the years through the efforts of many people. The Chassis Number List is based on factory records, and is largely the work of Dr. Brett Johnson, who has undertaken a crusade to compile the definitive 356 Serial Number Chart. He has succeeded in garnering arcane information from sources around the world and has added greatly to the reservoir of information now available to 356 enthusiasts. Aiding and abetting him are thousands of owners who have forwarded unique information about their own cars. Separate surveys have been compiled by Harry Pellow and others who deal with early Porsches on a daily basis, and the information from these sources is a valuable adjunct to a list such as this. The cooperation of the Porsche factory in researching their archives has, of course, been an invaluable asset, but a distance in time of three or four decades makes the quest that much harder. Brett's list has been updated at irregular intervals but recent information from the factory has filled in many blanks and the list is now as comprehensive as it probably ever will be.

The Carrera Engine List is the first definitive list of its type and comes from Olaf Lang in the Technical Services department at Porsche AG. Other individuals around the globe have also diligently researched the four-cam family and their efforts are reflected in this list.

Year	Vehicle and Engine Model Designation		Engine Model	Crankcase/ Bearing Type	Carburetors	Stroke/ Bore (mm)	Comp Ratio	Hp (DIN) @ rpm	Engine Serial Number
1950	**356**	356/1100	369	2 PB	32 PBI	64/73.5	7.0:1	40 @ 4200	0101 - 0411
1951		356/1100	369	2 PB	32 PBI	64/73.5	7.0:1	40 @ 4200	0412 - 0999 10001 - 10137
		356/1300	506	2 PB	32 PBI	64/80	6.5:1	44 @ 4200	1001 - 1099 20001 - 20821
	From Oct.	356/1500	527	2 RB	40 PBIC	74/80	7.0:1	60 @ 5000	30001 - 30737
1952		356/1100	369	2 PB	32 PBI	64/73.5	7.0:1	40 @ 4200	10138 - 10151
		356/1300	506	2 PB	32 PBI	64/80	6.5:1	44 @ 4200	20822 - 21297
	Until Nov.	356/1500	527	2 RB	40 PBIC	74/80	7.0:1	60 @ 5000	30738 - 30750
	From Aug.	356/1500	546	2 PB	32 PBI	74/80	7.0:1	55 @ 4400	30751 - 31025
	From July	356/1500 S	528	2 RB	40 PBIC	74/80	8.2:1	70 @ 5000	40001 - 40117
1953		356/1100	369	2 PB	32 PBI	64/73.5	7.0:1	40 @ 4200	10152 - 10161
		356/1300	506	2 PB	32 PBI	64/80	6.5:1	44 @ 4200	21298 - 21636
		356/1500	546	2 PB	32 PBI	74/80	7.0:1	55 @ 4400	31026 - 32569
		356/1500 S	528	2 RB	40 PBIC	74/80	8.2:1	70 @ 5000	40118 - 40685
	From Sept.	356/1300 S	589	2 RB	32 PBI	74/74.5	8.2:1	60 @ 5500	50001 - 50017
1954		356/1000	369	2 PB	32 PBI	64/73.5	7.0:1	40 @ 4200	10162 - 10199
		356/1300	506	2 PB	32 PBI	64/80	6.5:1	44 @ 4200	21637 - 21780
	Until Nov.	356/1300 S	589	2 RB	32 PBI	74/74.5	8.2:1	60 @ 5500	50018 - 50099
	July to Nov.	356/1300 A	506/1	2 PB	32 PBI	74/74.5	6.5:1	44 @ 4200	21781 - 21999
	Until Dec.	356/1500	546	2 PB	32 PBI	74/80	7.0:1	55 @ 4400	32570 - 33899
	Until Dec.	356/1500 S	528	2 RB	40 PBIC	74/80	8.2:1	70 @ 5000	40686 - 40999
	From Nov.	356/1300	506/2	3 PB	32 PBI	74/74.5	6.5:1	44 @ 4200	22001 - 22021
	From Dec.	356/1300 S	589/2	3 RB	32 PBIC*	74/74.5	7.5:1	60 @ 5500	50101 - 50127
		356/1500	546/2	3 PB	32 PBI	74/80	7.0:1	55 @ 4400	33901 - 34119
		356/1500 S	528/2	3 RB	40 PBIC	74/80	8.2:1	70 @ 5000	41001 - 41048
1955	Until Oct.	356/1300	506/2	3 PB	32 PBI	74/74.5	6.5:1	44 @ 4200	22022 - 22245
		356/1300 S	589/2	3 RB	32 PBIC*	74/74.5	7.5:1	60 @ 5500	50101 - 50127
	From July	Carrera 1500	547	RB	40 PII-4	66/85	9.5:1	110 @ 6200	90001 - 90096
		356/1500	546/2	3 PB	32 PBI	74/80	7.0:1	55 @ 4400	34120 - 35790
		356/1500 S	528/2	3 RB	40 PBIC	74/80	8.2:1	70 @ 5000	41049 - 41999
	From Oct.	356A/1300	506/2	3 PB	32 PBI	74/74.5	6.5:1	44 @ 4200	22246 - 22273
	356A	356A/1300 S	589/2	3 RB	32 PBIC*	74/74.5	7.5:1	60 @ 5500	50128 - 50135
	From Nov.	Carrera 1500 GS	547/1	RB	40 PII-4	66/85	9.0:1	100 @ 6200	90501 - 90959
		Carrera 1500 GT	547/1	RB	40 PII-4	66/85	9.0:1	110 @ 6200	90501 - 90959
	From Oct.	356A/1600	616/1	3 PB	32 PBIC	74/82.5	7.5:1	60 @ 4500	60001 - 60608
	From Sept.	356A/1600 S	616/2	3 RB	40 PBIC	74/82.5	8.5:1	75 @ 5000	80001 - 80110
1956		356A/1300	506/2	3 PB	32 PBI	74/74.5	6.5:1	44 @ 4200	22274 - 22471
		356A/1300 S	589/2	3 RB	32 PBIC*	74/74.5	7.5:1	60 @ 5500	50136 - 50155
		Carrera 1500 GS	547/1	RB	40 PII-4	66/85	9.0:1	100 @ 6200	90501 - 90959
		Carrera 1500 GT	547/1	RB	40 PII-4	66/85	9.0:1	110 @ 6200	90501 - 90959
		356A/1600	616/1	3 PB	32 PBIC	74/82.5	7.5:1	60 @ 4500	60609 - 63926
		356A/1600 S	616/2	3 RB	40 PBIC	74/82.5	8.5:1	75 @ 5000	80111 - 80756

Year	Reutter Coupe	Karmann Coupe	Karmann Hardtop	Reutter Cabriolet	Heuer Cabriolet	Speedster	Convertible D	Roadster
1950	5002 – 5013 5017 – 5018 5020 – 5026 5029 – 5032 5034 – 5104 5163 – 5410			5014 – 5015 5033 5115 5131	5001 5019 5027 – 5028 5105 – 5114 5116 – 5130			
1951	5411 – 5600 10531 – 11280			5132 – 5138 10001 – 10165	5139 – 5162 10351 – 10432			
1952	11301 – 12084			10166 – 10211 10251 – 10350 15011 – 15050	10433 – 10469 12301 – 12387 (Latter series includes America Roadsters)			
1953	50001 – 51231			15051 – 15116 60001 – 60394				
1954	51232 – 52531			60395 – 60722		80001 – 80200 (12223 = 80001)		
1955	52532 – 54223			60723 – 61000		80201 – 81234		
	55001 – 55390			61001 – 61069		81901 – 82000		
1956	55391 – 58311			61070 – 61499		82001 – 83156		

Year	Vehicle and Engine Model Designation		Engine Model	Crankcase/ Bearing Type	Carburetors	Stroke/ Bore (mm)	Comp. Ratio	Hp (DIN) @ rpm	Engine Serial Number
1957	Until Aug.	356A/1300	506/2	3 PB	32 PBI	74/74.5	6.5:1	44 @ 4200	22472 – 22999
		356A/1300 S	589/2	3 RB	32 PBIC*	74/74.5	7.5:1	60 @ 5500	50156 – 50999
		Carrera 1500 GS	547/1	RB	40 PII-4	66/85	9.0:1	100 @ 6200	90501 – 90959
		Carrera 1500 GT	547/1	RB	40 PII-4	66/85	9.0:1	110 @ 6200	90501 – 90959
		356A/1600	616/1	3 PB	32 PBIC	74/82.5	7.5:1	60 @ 4500	63927 – 66999
		356A/1600S	616/2	3 RB	40 PBIC	74/82.5	8.5:1	75 @ 5000	80757 – 81199
	From Sept. **356A T-2**	Carrera 1500 GS	547/1	RB	40 PII-4	66/85	9.0:1	100 @ 6200	90501 – 90959
		Carrera 1500 GT	547/1	RB	40 PII-4	66/85	9.0:1	110 @ 6200	90501 – 90959
		356A/1600	616/1	3 PB	32 NDIX	74/82.5	7.5:1	60 @ 4500	67001 – 68216
		356A/1600 S	616/2	3 PB	32 NDIX	74/82.5	8.5:1	75 @ 5000	81201 – 81521
1958		356A/1600	616/1	3 PB	32 NDIX	74/82.5	7.5:1	60 @ 4500	68217 – 72468
		356A/1600 S	616/2	3 PB	32 NDIX	74/82.5	8.5:1	75 @ 5000	81522 – 83145
	From May	Carrera 1500 GT	692/0	RB	40 PII-4	66/85	9.0:1	110 @ 6400	91001 – 91037
			692/1	PB	40 PII-4	66/85	9.0:1	110 @ 6400	92001 – 92014
	From Aug.	Carrera 1600 GS	692/2	PB	40 PII-4	66/87.5	9.5:1	105 @ 6500	93001 – 93065
1959	From Feb.	Carrera 1600 GT	692/3	PB	W 40 DCM	66/87.5	9.8:1	115 @ 6500	95001 – 95114
	Until Sept.	356A/1600	616/1	3 PB	32 NDIX	74/82.5	7.5:1	60 @ 4500	72469 – 79999
		356A/1600 S	616/2	3 PB	32 NDIX	74/82.5	8.5:1	75 @ 5000	83146 – 84770
	From Sept. **356B T-5**	356B/1600	616/1	3 PB	32 NDIX	74/82.5	7.5:1	60 @ 4500	600101 – 601500
		356B/1600 S	616/2	3 PB	32 NDIX	74/82.5	8.5:1	75 @ 5000	84771 – 85550
		356B/1600 S-90	616/7	3 PB	40 PII-4	74/82.5	9.0:1	90 @ 5500	800101 – 802000
		Carrera 1600 GS	692/2	PB	40 PII-4	66/87.5	9.5:1	105 @ 6500	93101 – 93138
		Carrera 1600 GT	692/3	PB	W 40 DCM	66/87.5	9.8:1	115 @ 6500	95001 – 95114
1960		356B/1600	616/1	3 PB	32 NDIX	74/82.5	7.5:1	60 @ 4500	601501 – 604700
		356B/1600 S	616/2	3 PB	32 NDIX	74/82.5	8.5:1	75 @ 5000	85551 – 88320
		356B/1600 S-90	616/7	3 PB	40 PII-4	74/82.5	9.0:1	90 @ 5500	800101 – 802000
		Carrera 1600 GT	692/3	PB	W 40 DCM	66/87.5	9.8:1	115 @ 6500	95001 – 95114
			692/3A	PB	44 PII-4	66/87.5	9.8:1	134 @ 7300	96001 – 96050
1961	Until Sept.	356B/1600	616/1	3 PB	32 NDIX	74/82.5	7.5:1	60 @ 4500	604701 – 606799
		356B/1600 S	616/2	3 PB	32 NDIX	74/82.5	8.5:1	75 @ 5000	88321 – 89999
									085001 – 085670
		356B/1600 S-90	616/7	3 PB	40 PII-4	74/82.5	9.0:1	90 @ 5500	802001 – 803999
		Carrera 1600 GT	692/3A	PB	44 PII-4	66/87.5	9.8:1	134 @ 7300	96001 – 96050
	From Sept. From Aug. **356B T-6**	356B/1600	616/1	3 PB	32 NDIX	74/82.5	7.5:1	60 @ 4500	606801 – 607750
		356B/1600 S	616/12	3 PB	32 NDIX	74/82.5	8.5:1	75 @ 5000	700001 – 701200
		356B/1600 S-90	616/7	3 PB	40 PII-4	74/82.5	9.0:1	90 @ 5500	804001 – 804630
1962	Until July	356B/1600	616/1	3 PB	32 NDIX	74/82.5	7.5:1	60 @ 4500	607751 – 608900
		356B/1600 S	616/12	3 PB	32 NDIX	74/82.5	8.5:1	75 @ 5000	701201 – 702800
		356B/1600 S-90	616/7	3 PB	40 PII-4	74/82.5	9.0:1	90 @ 5500	804631 – 805600
		Carrera 2/2000 GS	587/1	PB	40 PII-4	74/92	9.2:1	130 @ 6200	97001 – 97446
	From July	356B/1600	616/1	3 PB	32 NDIX	74/82.5	7.5:1	60 @ 4500	608901 – 610000
		356B/1600 S	616/12	3 PB	32 NDIX	74/82.5	8.5:1	75 @ 5000	702801 – 705050
		356B/1600 S-90	616/7	3 PB	40 PII-4	74/82.5	9.0:1	90 @ 5500	805601 – 806600

Year	Reutter Coupe	Karmann Coupe	Karmann Hardtop	Reutter Cabriolet	Heuer Cabriolet	Speedster	Convertible D	Roadster
1957	58312 - 59099 100001 - 101692			61500 - 61892		83201 -83791		
	101693 - 102504			150001 - 150149		83792 - 84370		
1958	102505 - 106174			150150 - 151531		84371 - 84922	85501 - 85886	
1959	106175 - 108917			151532 - 152475		84923 - 84954	85887 - 86830	
	108918 - 110237			152476 - 152943				86831 - 87391
1960	110238 - 114650			152944 - 154560				87392 - 88920
1961	114651 - 117476		200001 - 201048	154561 - 155569				88921 - 89010 Drauz 89011 - 89483 D'Ieteren
	117601 - 118950		201601 - 202200	155601 - 156200				89601 - 89849
1962	118951 - 121099	210001 - 210899	202201 - 202299	156201 - 156999				
	121100 - 123042	210900 - 212171		157000 - 157768				

Year	Vehicle and Engine Model Designation			Engine Model	Crankcase/ Bearing Type	Carburetors	Stroke/ Bore (mm)	Comp. Ratio	Hp (DIN) @ rpm	Engine Serial Number
1963	Until July		356B/1600	616/1	3 PB	32 NDIX	74/82.5	7.5:1	60 @ 4500	610001 – 611000 0600501 – 0600600 611001 – 611200**
			356B/1600 S	616/12	3 PB	32 NDIX	74/82.5	8.5:1	75 @ 5000	705051 – 706000 0700501 – 0701200 706001 – 707200**
			356B/1600 S-90	616/7	3 PB	40 PII-4	74/82.5	9.0:1	90 @ 5500	806601 – 807000 0800501 – 0801000 807001 – 8074000**
			Carrera 2/2000 GS	587/1	PB	40 PII-4	74/92	9.2:1	130 @ 6200	97001 – 97446
			Carrera 2/2000 GT	587/2	PB	W 46 IDM/2	74/92	9.8:1	160 @ 6900	98001 – 98032
	From July 356C		356C/1600 C	616/15	3 PB	32 NDIX	74/82.5	8.5:1	75 @ 5200	710001 – 711870 730001–731102**
			356C/1600 SC	616/16	3 PB	40 PII-4	74/82.5	9.5:1	95 @ 5800	810001 – 811001 820001 – 820522**
1964			356C/1600 C	616/15	3 PB	32 NDIX	74/82.5	8.5:1	75 @ 5200	711871 – 716804 731103 – 733027**
			356C/1600 SC	616/16	3 PB	40 PII-4	74/82.5	9.5:1	95 @ 5800	811002 – 813562 820523 – 821701**
			Carrera 2/2000 GS	587/1	PB	40 PII-4	74/92	9.2:1	130 @ 6200	97001 – 97446
1965			356C/1600 C	616/15	3 PB	32 NDIX	74/82.5	8.5:1	75 @ 5200	716805 – 717899 733028 – 733197**
			356C/1600 SC	616/16	3 PB	40 PII-4	74/82.5	9.5:1	95 @ 5800	813563 – 813893 821702 – 821855**
1966	March		356C/1600 SC	616/16	3 PB	40 PII-4	74/82.5	9.5:1	95 @ 5800	813894 – 813903

PB: Plain journal bearings
RB: Roller bearings

2: Two-piece crankcase
3: Three-piece crankcase

* 589/2 1300S engines were also equipped with 40 PBIC carburetors

** equipped with new heater system

Year	Reutter Coupe	Karmann Coupe	Karmann Hardtop	Reutter Cabriolet	Heuer Cabriolet	Speedster	Convertible D	Roadster
1963	123043 – 125239	212172 – 214400		157769 – 158700				
	126001 – 128104	215001 – 216738		159001 – 159832				
1964	128105 – 131927	216739 – 221482		159833 – 161577				
1965	131928 – 131930	221483 – 222580		161578 – 162165				
1966				162166 – 162175				

356 Exchange Chassis

In addition to the standard 356 series, there were three series of exchange chassis for various cars, including race cars, prototypes and random production cars. These chassis numbers do not necessarily correlate to any particular model or type.

Years	**Chassis Number**
1953-1961	12201-12376
1958-1962	5601-5624
1959-1965	13001-13414

Four-Cam Engine Specifications and Serial Numbers

Compiled by Olaf Lang, Porsche AG, May 1991

Type	Year	Car Type	cc	Bore	Stroke	Comp. Ratio	Hp (DIN) @ rpm	Bearing Type	Car- buretors	Motor Number
547	1953–1954	Spyder 550–1100	1098	73	66	9.5:1	93 @ 5500	RB	S 40 PII-4	Prototype
547	1953–1956	Spyder 550A, 356 Carrera	1498	85	66	9.5:1	110 @ 6200	RB	S 40 PII-4	90001–90096
547/1	1954–1955	"Werks" Spyder 550 Le Mans	1300	80	66	8.0:1	93 @ 5500	RB	S 40 P11-4	Prototype
547/1	1955–1958	356A Carrera GS and GT	1498	85	66	9.0:1	100 @ 6200 GS/ 110 @ 6200GT	RB	S 40 PII-4	90501–90959
547/2	1955–1958	Spyder 550A 1500 RS	1498	85	66	9.8:1	135 @ 7200	RB	W 40 DCM	90102–90149
547/3	1958–1960	Spyder RSK 1500, Type 718	1498	85	66	10.0:1	150 @ 7800	RB	W 46 IDM	90200–90229
547/3	1960–1961	Spyder RS 60/61	1500	85	66	10.0:1	150 @ 7800	RB	W 46 IDM	90250–90264
547/3	1959–1961	F1, F2	1500	85	66	10.4:1	164 @ 8000	RB	W 46 IDM	Prototype
547/4	1959	Spyder RSK 1600,Type 718	1587	87.5	66	10.0:1	160 @ 7800	RB	W 46 IDM	90230–90232
547/4	1960–1961	Spyder RS 60/61 1600, Type 718	1587	87.5	66	10.0:1	160 @ 7600	RB	W 46 IDM	90300–90338
547/4	1962	Spyder replacement motors	1587	87.5	66	10.0:1	165 @ 7800	RB	W 46 IDM	90339–90340
547/5	1962	Spyder replacement motors	1678	90	66	10.0:1	170 @ 7900	RB	W 46 IDM	90400–90405
547/5	1962	Spyder replacement motor	1678	90	66	10.0:1	180 @ 7900	RB	W 46 IDM	90406–90408
547/5A	1963–1964	Porsche-Elva	1708	90	66	10.0:1	175 @ 7900	RB	W 46 IDM	90411–90428
547/6	1961	F1	1500	85	66	10.4:1	164 @ 8000	RB	W 46 IDM	Prototype
547/6	1961–1963	Spyder RS62	1760	91	66	10.0:1	185 @ 7900	RB	W 46 IDM	90450–90455
719/0	1958	Experimental, F1	1498	85	66	10.0:1	155 @ 7200	RB	D. Injection	Prototype
719/1	1958	"Werks" Spyder, Type 718, F1	1498	85	66	10.0:1	162 @ 7800	RB	W 46 IDM	Prototype
719/2	1959	"Werks" Spyder, Type 718, F1	1498	85	66	10.0:1	160 @ 8000	RB	W 46 IDM	Prototype
719/3	1960	"Werks" RS 60	1587	87.5	66	10.0:1	160 @ 8000	RB	W 46 JDM	Prototype
719/4	1960	"Werks" RS 60	1678	90	66	10.0:1	170 @ 8000	RB	W 46 JDM	Prototype
692/0	1958	356A Carrera GT	1498	85	66	9.0:1	110 @ 6400	RB	S 40 PII-4	91001–91037
692/1	1958	356A Carrera GT	1498	85	66	9.0:1	110 @ 6400	PB	S 40 PII-4	92001–92014
692/2	1958–1959	356A and 356B Carrera GS	1587	87.5	66	9.5:1	105 @ 6500	PB	S 40 PII-4	93001–93062
692/2	1959	356B Carrera GS	1587	87.5	66	9.5:1	105 @ 6500	PB	S 40 PII-4	93100–93138
692/3	1959–1960	356B Carrera GT	1587	87.5	66	9.8:1	115 @ 6500	PB	W 40 DCM/3	95001–95114
692/3A	1960–1961	356B Carrera GT, Abarth GTL	1587	87.5	66	9.8:1	135 @ 7300	PB	S 44 PII-4	96001–96050
587/1	1962–1964	356B and 356C Carrera 2 GS	1966	92	74	9.2:1	130 @ 6200	PB	S 40 PII-4	97001–97446
587/2	1963	356B Carrera 2 GT	1966	92	74	9.8:1	160 @ 6300	PB	W 46 IDM/2	98005–98032
587/3	1964	GTS 904, Carrera 2 GT "Scraper"	1966	92	74	9.8:1	180 @ 6900	PB	W 46 IDM/2	99001–99026
587/3	1964	GTS 904	1966	92	74	9.8:1	180 @ 7200	PB	S 44 PII-4 (W 46 IDM)	99027–99106
587/3	1964	Porsche-Elva	1966	92	74	9.8:1	185 @ 7200	PB	S 44 PII-4 (W 46 IDM)	99104–99105

Index

Le Mans, June 1952

Like the tortoise and the hare, Gmünd coupe number 50 is passed by a V-8 powered Cunningham sports car from American Briggs Cunningham. The diminutive Porsches showed that speed was second-ary to toughness, but in a few years the Stuttgart entries would evolve from turtle to rabbit and, eventually, to overall winner. Tom Countryman